Get It Right
First Time

A self help and training guide to
project management

Peter James

Russell House Publishing

First published in 2004 by:
Russell House Publishing Ltd.
4 St. George's House
Uplyme Road
Lyme Regis
Dorset DT7 3LS

Tel: 01297-443948
Fax: 01297-442722
e-mail: help@russellhouse.co.uk
www.russellhouse.co.uk

British Library Cataloguing-in-publication Data:
A catalogue record for this book is available from the British Library.

ISBN: 1-903855-12-8

Printed by J W Arrowsmith, Bristol

About Russell House Publishing

RHP is a group of social work, probation, education and youth and community work practitioners and academics working in collaboration with a professional publishing team. Our aim is to work closely with the field to produce innovative and valuable materials to help managers, trainers, practitioners and students. We are keen to receive feedback on publications and new ideas for future projects. For details of our other publications please visit our website or ask us for a catalogue. Contact details are on this page.

Contents

Acknowledgements

Firstly I have to acknowledge the many people, clients, colleagues and delegates who have enlightened me so much over the past twenty years. The good thing about working in training and consultancy is that it is a continuous learning process. Many people in that time have given me access to notes, files and other useful material and this book could not have been written without their help.

I am also indebted to the critical readers, Hilary Corrick, Kathy Estcourt, Ian Hughes and my son Chris who did an excellent job.

Finally, thanks to my wife Ann, who first suggested the book and who has supported me, cajoled me and advised me throughout the project, especially through the difficult times.

Peter James

Foreword

Being involved in a project, whether as a project manager or a team member — or even just being one of the people that the project affects, can be a rewarding experience. Equally, it can be a stressful and soul destroying time for all participants.

It is more to do with the way that the project is managed than whether or not the objectives are desirable. I've been to many wedding receptions that were so badly arranged that going home time couldn't come soon enough. On the other hand I recall being made redundant when my son was just a month old — and to this day I have nothing but good feelings about the way the whole issue was handled — even though I lost a job in which I was very happy.

Near to where I live is a special needs school with a track record of high achievement — Beacon Status, Investors in People — you name it — they've got it. The school needed to move out of their premises into temporary accommodation for three months to enable improvements to be made. The idea of appointing a project manager was mooted. The Head decided that this was an unnecessary expense.

When the move took place there was a catalogue of errors: telephones not working; door handles not fitted to suit the children's physical limitations; no safety door locking system in place; on the day of the move the staff carrying their own belongings and furniture from one building to the other; electricity not on by the day of the move — just to name a few. In a nutshell — no co-ordination, no attention to detail. The result was a severe drop in staff morale and co-operation and the next staff meeting was heated to say the least.

At the meeting the Head recognised the difficulties that had occurred and vowed that on the move back into the re-furbished premises these issues would not arise. 'We shall learn from these mistakes' she said. And they will. They are a very competent team of people and the *next* move will go well and morale will pick up again. But they are fortunate that they have — in effect — a second shot at getting it right — a chance to make amends — a chance to prove they are a competent group of people. The first move, however, will always remain as a bad memory.

We can all (well, nearly all) get things right second time. The trick is to get them right first time — because in most projects there is only the one shot at it. This book is a guide to delivering successful projects — **First Time**.

The techniques covered can be used for projects in any field of operation and for projects of any size or duration. The book is based on material that has been successfully used in the training and development of people from all areas of the business and service industry spectrum over the past twenty years.

Throughout the book there are a series of exercises with some suggested answers. There are also examples showing the use of specific techniques. All this material is deliberately non-specific so the reader can adapt the material to suit their own particular circumstances. For example the chart using building a house could just have easily been produced to introduce a complaints procedure; set up an older persons' home; implement government legislation or open a new youth club to name a few.

The book is in three parts. Part 1 is an overview of project management. Part 2 deals with core project management techniques and sets out a three-part template for successful project management. Part 3 deals with some general problem solving and management techniques that are widely used by successful project managers. The book is set out so that the reader can use it as a self help guide or as the basis for formal training or simply as a text book.

Section 1

Projects and Project Management

Chapter 1

The Nature of Projects

Project management versus process management

The two basic ways of managing situations are by process management and by project management.

Process management

Process management is the way we manage things that have been through a development stage (a project) and are now sorted, organised, and in a form with which we are happy. When we reach this stage, i.e. when we have solved all the problems and are happy that we have settled on an agreed method for delivering our product or service, we can write procedures for people to follow, we can train people in the correct methods to use and we can put specific checks and balances in place to ensure that the same process is followed every time. The idea is that by following the same process every time we shall get the same desired result every time.

Process management is designed to handle the **standard** case. It is the way we manage the manufacture of cars and washing machines. It is the way we run offices using systems and procedures. It is the way people are handled by call centres. It is the way we are managed when we visit a hospital, the town hall, the supermarket. The problem is that whilst process management is the most effective method from a management point of view it is not particularly comfortable at the receiving end.

People do not enjoy being **processed**.

Project management

When the situation that is to be managed involves dealing with the new or the unknown, or the one-off situation, then a different approach is needed. These situations may include problem solving, or arranging a one-off event such as a conference, an important meeting or a training course. Or the situation may be that we are dealing with clients where we do not want them to feel that they are being 'processed', where they need to feel that they are special and their particular problem or issue is special. This is where project management techniques come into their own.

Project management is a standard way of dealing with non-standard situations. It is a process for dealing with situations that have yet to become 'processes'. Project management is a system that provides a template for bringing 'order' into new and unknown situations.

Project management techniques can be of great use in any problem solving situation. They are also very effective to use when faced with fast changing situations – such as managing a rapidly expanding and fast moving organisation. They are particularly useful when dealing with any situations involving partnerships or inter-agency working, such as in the care industry and they are ideal for people involved in case management where a 'personal' feel is essential.

Most important of all is the fact that successful project management techniques are designed to promote the involvement, commitment and co-operation of all parties – otherwise known as 'joined up' management.

What is a project?

At various times in your life, you will have been involved in projects.
Typical examples of projects include:

- Case management e.g. social work cases or legal cases.
- Planning a conference or seminar.
- Solving organisational or procedural problems.
- Renovating an old house.
- Organising an event e.g. a wedding or a party.
- Putting on a play.
- Building a kit car.

A project definition

A project is the action taken to **change** something usually because someone has identified:

- a problem
- an opportunity

A problem can be any set of circumstances which, if left unresolved, will put at risk the credibility or profitability of an organisation. One example might be the failure of a social work unit to identify that a young person needs help. Another might be a risk that might adversely affect the future success of an organisation e.g. bad publicity. Or, perhaps, it can be an opportunity that has been spotted e.g. applying for National Lottery funding – which must be acted upon before a rival group seizes the chance.

Some people are loath to think of their clients as problems or, worse still, opportunities. However, that is what they are. This is not to say that clients themselves are problems but their circumstances or their behaviour is usually the problem or opportunity that needs addressing.

Typical reasons for projects are:

- To improve the service to customers or clients.
- To respond to or counter the activities of competitors.
- To respond to external changes such as the development of new technology
- To improve morale; to exploit a gap in the market.
- To fill a social need; to improve internal processes.
- To respond to government initiative or new laws.

Project characteristics

All projects have certain characteristics, namely:

- A defined change.
- A specified cost.
- A set start and finish date.
- An agreed quality standard or specification.
- There is no rehearsal.
- Many disciplines are involved.
- Different levels of staff are likely to be involved.
- There may be many sub-projects within the overall project.
- Projects are non-routine and usually involve the new or unknown.

 Not all projects or assignments have all of the above characteristics but most projects will have – even though at first glance they may not be apparent.

Are all projects the same?

Taking a young person into care and planning their future protection and development is not the same as organising a conference, a training course or the office Xmas party. Re-locating the entire youth offending team to a new location is not the same as tidying one's office, but they are all projects. So are these projects all the same and if not what are the differences?

All projects are different in that they each have a unique outcome, or 'deliverable'. They are all different when it comes to the specifics, the details, the steps that need to be taken in order to reach the goal. They are different too in the order in which things happen. For some projects there needs to be a feasibility study (a mini-project) at the start in order to establish whether a larger project is justified. In other cases the justification already exists so the project is all about delivery and not much about problem solving. For some projects the project team must be assembled at the very start of the project, whereas in other cases the team can be put together gradually as the project develops. Some projects need tight, formal control – others can be run fairly loosely. Some projects unfold in a fairly logical and orderly way – others do not – not necessarily because they are badly managed – but because the nature of the project makes it difficult to resolve and therefore there is a certain amount of 'back to the drawing board' activity.

All successful projects are the same in that they all have:

- a project manager
- a project team of some description
- a customer
- a deliverable
- a specific reason and purpose
- a series of identifiable steps
- a defined timescale

Project complexity

Projects need not be large to qualify as projects. The two key factors are:
- Change is involved.
- A problem or opportunity is involved.

Some things that might be different include:
- Size/number of separate activities.
- The number of different skills or departments/people involved.
- The amount of time involved.
- The amount of money involved.
- The number of different activities involved.
- The impact on the company/organisation, its customers and employees.
- More complicated control procedures may be needed.
- It may be harder to communicate.

The things that will be the same are:
- There will be a goal – or deliverable – and a customer.
- There will be a project team and a project manager.
- There will be plans.
- There will be definable project stages.
- There will be control and review procedures.

So all projects, large or small, follow a set routine or pattern, only the complexity of the planning and control procedures differ.

Why some projects fail

Think of all the projects in which you have been involved. Which ones were successful and which ones failed? And why did they fail?

Most failed projects have some of the following characteristics:
- The project is not finished in time.
- The project budget is overspent.
- The project solution doesn't work.
- At the end of the project you still have the original problem.
- At the end of the project the original problem has gone but you have many other, worse problems.
- The project is badly co-ordinated. People don't know exactly what is expected of them.
- People aren't committed to the project – they think it is a bad idea.
- The project manager is not a good administrator.

- The project manager is not good with people.
- The project changes direction several times.
- The people affected don't know what is going on.
- Additional work is done but the cost of the work was not recovered from the client.
- Funding has to be 'borrowed' from another budget.
- At the end of the project there are bad feelings and scores to settle amongst the participants.

The above list, although not exhaustive, is clearly one to avoid when managing your own projects.

The key ingredients for project success

For successful projects you need:
- a well defined objective
- a well thought out solution, guaranteed to solve the real problem
- a systematic approach
- effective communication
- committed people who know what is going on

Let us deal with each of these.

Having a well-defined objective appears to be a simple task. In practice it is extremely difficult. Many projects are well under way before the objective has been really clarified. Remembering the SMART acronym will help with this process.

The objective must be:
- **S**pecific
- **M**easurable
- **A**ttainable and Agreed
- **R**ealistic
- **T**imely

Often the objective will become clearer as you determine the real problem. Many projects are carried out to solve what is thought to be the problem when in fact it is only a symptom.

 Example

Traffic wardens exist to prevent illegal parking in congested areas but suppose our public transport system was free, efficient, reliable, clean and safe, would we still have as many people using cars? And would we then need traffic wardens?

A systematic approach means that all projects should be:

- auditable – how was the project managed and controlled?
- measurable – were the success criteria met?

In order to be able to audit a project there must be a stated methodology or procedure for running the project. The methodology or system can be complex and all embracing and usually is on major projects or it can be basic and simple if the project is small – you can choose. Once you have stated the method you will use to run the project it is then easy for an independent person to assess whether or not you have followed the agreed method.

Your project can only be measured if you have produced and published plans. Here again the plans can be complex or simple depending on the complexity of the project, but you must have plans, dates, timings, costs, performance criteria in order that your project can be measured.

Effective communication is a meaningless phrase unless quantified or qualified in some way – so let us look at the statement 'committed people who know what is going on'. Turn this around. People who 'know what is going on' are often committed. The project manager should keep people 'in the picture' by involving them as much as possible, by devolving information to the appropriate people at the appropriate time, through meetings, plans, progress reports and sometimes by simply being available. Usually this will result in them being 'on side' or 'buying into the project' to use two common phrases. If this happens, then it can be said that there is effective communication.

Chapter 2
The Key Project Stages

Most projects, large or small, have clearly defined stages. Each stage is a mini-project or sub-project. There are three essential stages in a project:

- **Clarification stage:** where you clarify what you are trying to achieve and decide in broad terms how you are going to achieve it.

- **Planning stage:** where you plan in detail what you are going to do, the resources you are going to need, the timescales and the costs.

- **Delivery stage:** where you carry out the plan right through to project delivery, project closure and project review.

We can depict the three stages as shown below:

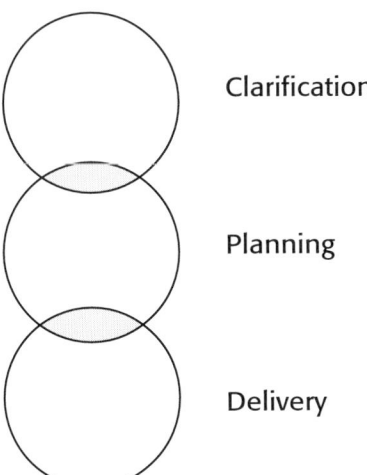

Clarification

Planning

Delivery

Figure 2.1

Notice that the circles overlap. This is because in real life the stages overlap.

It is not possible to do project clarification without some of the planning falling into place. Similarly, when doing detailed planning, it sometimes is necessary to go back and modify the solution agreed at stage one. It is not always necessary to complete the planning stage before commencing on some of the work. Also, as work is in progress, things will occur that make it necessary to re-visit the planning stage. It is an iterative process, i.e. you do it over and over again as required.

Now let us examine each stage in more detail.

The clarification stage

Define the problem or opportunity:

- What are the symptoms?
- What are the possible causes?
- Draw a cause and effect diagram (discussed later).
- What is the cause?
- What are we trying to achieve?
- What is the real problem?

Collect evidence:

- facts and figures
- judgements and observations
- other people's opinions

Generate ideas:

- think creatively
- find all the alternatives

The planning stage

Plan:

- What scope have we got?
- What is the best thing to do for now/in the long term?
- How will it affect other people?
- What resources will be needed?
  - materials
  - space
  - tools
  - skills
  - people
  - finance
  - time

Publish the plan and get it **signed off** by the people or person that commissioned the project and by the key players involved in the delivery of the project.

Getting a project signed off is not the same as getting the project agreed. Getting the project signed off means exactly that. The same principle applies to key moments elsewhere during the life of the project when these moments should be **signed off** too.

The delivery stage

Act:

- carry out the plan
- communicate progress effectively
- monitor changes and risks

Follow up:

Check the results against expectations i.e. audit the results and the method.

This logical approach may be applied to any projects or assignments or cases. It can help you to decide on the best action to take after an incident of indiscipline or it can help deal with people's personal problems. It can equally well be used to design an improved working method, introduce a new system, or design a new office layout to name a few.

There may be several planning or action stages in a large project. In each stage you have an activity or a number of activities – each with an end product or deliverable. It is easier to plan and control projects in short stages. If the stages are too long, they cannot be managed properly.

There should be an assessment at the end of each stage.

Although we depict the structure of a project as three equal circles the reality is that the project stages for a successful project usually look as shown below, with most of the work taking place during the clarification stage.

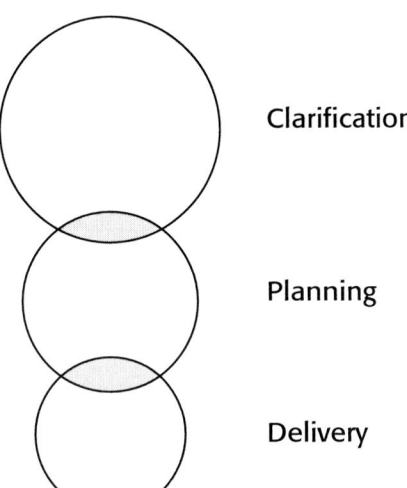

Figure 2.2

On the other hand unsuccessful projects usually look as shown in Figure 2.3, with little effort at the beginning resulting in the delivery stage being the time when many problems occur that have to be sorted.

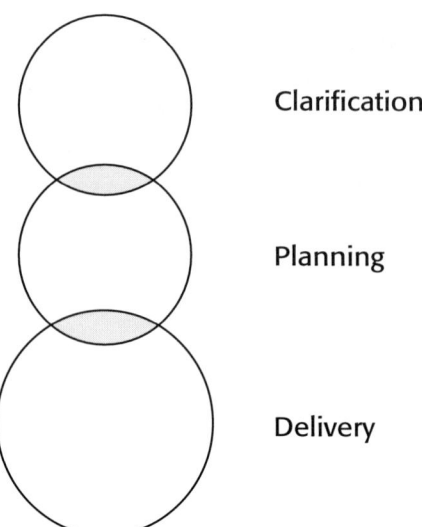

Clarification

Planning

Delivery

Figure 2.3

A very simple example could be that you have been asked to write a report about a problem of staff absenteeism in your department. Your diagram should probably look like Figure 2.2 on page 11, bearing in mind that most effort in producing written work should go into the research and planning.

Chapter 3
The Project Organisation Structure or Anatomy

At the start of a project, an organisation structure should be set up which defines for everyone:

- roles
- responsibilities
- reporting structure

Having the right structure for a project is important to ensure that everyone involved knows what is happening at every stage of the project, e.g. who is responsible for each aspect of the project or who to go to if there is a query. The project structure usually needs to be different from the structure that is in place to run the normal day-to-day activities of the organisation.

Work groups that consistently fail to get their projects done on time, within budget and correctly working, invariably have people involved in the projects who do not understand the project anatomy, or set up. Usually this is because no project organisation or anatomy has been defined.

 Example

A voluntary organisation had been asked to provide a volunteer to visit a secure unit on a regular basis to ensure the residents were cared for appropriately, that their needs were met and their human rights upheld. Unfortunately, the assistant manager of the unit who had been asked to run the project of implementation by her boss (project sponsor) did not set up the project appropriately in the first place. The staff involved were not told what was going on or what to expect – just that the scheme was being introduced. They were antagonistic towards the volunteer, tried to prevent her from visiting the site and when she did visit made her life very difficult. They often refused her requests for information or to see a particular young person and even when something as easy as a young person having access to a telephone was agreed it took a good deal of time before it was implemented.

After a 'clear the air' meeting it transpired that the role of both the volunteer and the staff involved had not been clearly defined or communicated so there was a lot of suspicion on both sides. Staff did not know how far they could go in providing access for the volunteer and no-one knew who to go to directly to get the volunteer's recommendations changed. There was no project organisation; roles and responsibilities were unclear.

What do we mean by set up?

Another way to look at it is this. A drama society decides to put on a pantomime – Cinderella – and calls a meeting to get things arranged. What is one of the first things to be decided?

Yes, it is who plays Cinderella, who plays Buttons, who will be the ugly sisters and who is getting the pumpkin and the white mice. We must decide all these things because if we do not we will arrive here next week to find three Cinderella's, two Buttons, no ugly sisters and no pumpkin or mice. It is obvious when we are talking about putting on Cinderella, but this simple principle is often overlooked on other, and often more important projects. Identifying key roles and responsibilities is fundamental to successful project management.

What is the right set up?

Let us look at a typical project and the way that it is set up.

We can see from Figure 3.1 that we have six key players – the project board, the sponsor, the customer/client, the users, the project manager and the project team. The role of this last important group is dealt with more fully in Section 3 of this book. Names are not too important here but an understanding of roles is vital. Let us consider the various roles and responsibilities of these inter-related groups.

Figure 3.1: Anatomy of a project

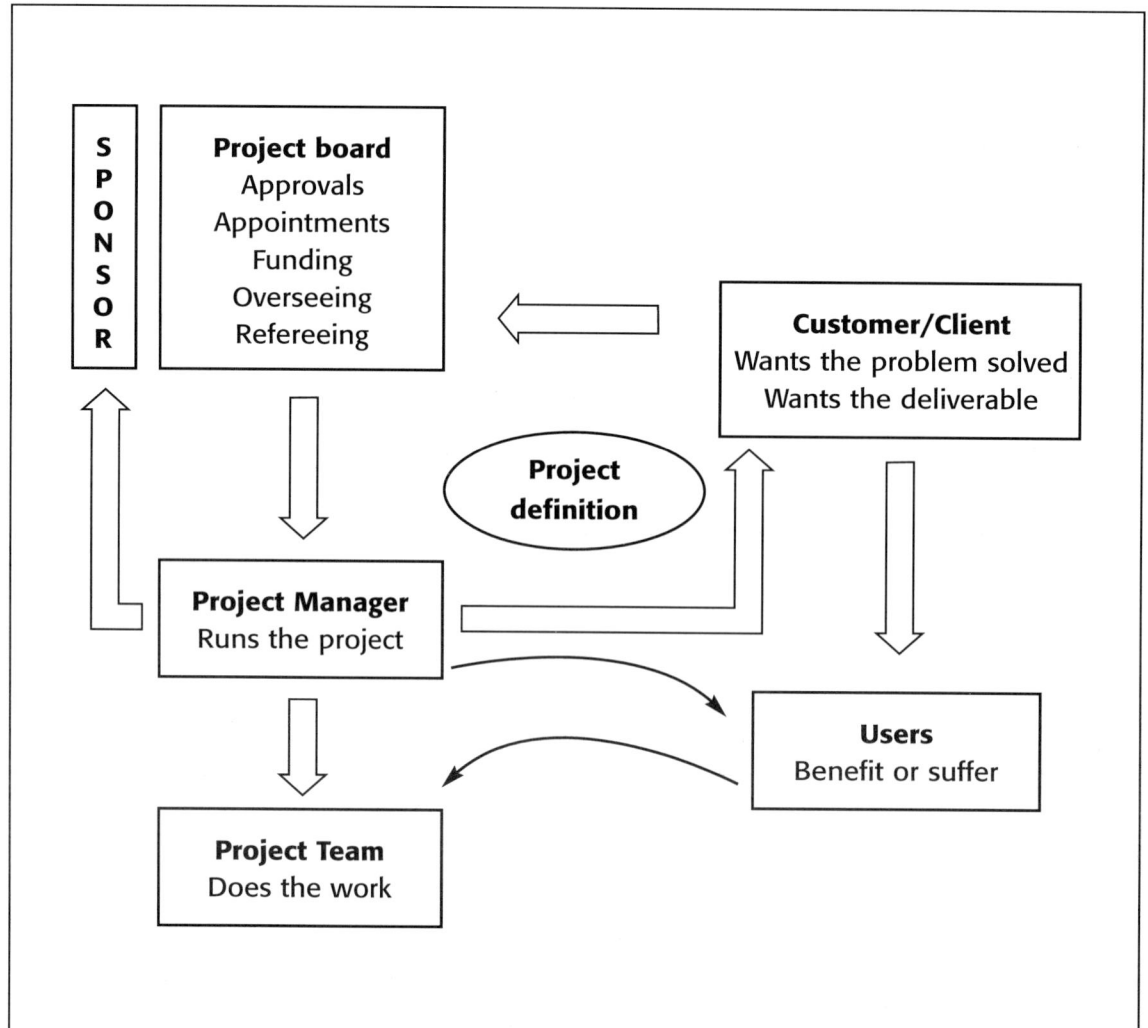

The project board

The project board is the person or, more usually, a group of people who manage a specific section of the organisation and make the key decisions about which activities they will allocate time, money and resources to. These people have ultimate control. Their job is to:

- Approve or reject project proposals.
- Appoint a project manager.
- Allocate or manage funds.
- Oversee the project.
- Referee if and when disputes occur.
- Nominate a sponsor or 'champion' for the project.

The sponsor

The sponsor, or project champion, is someone who will act as the contact point or go-between linking the project manager and the project board.

It is easier for the project manager to report to one person rather than try to report to a group of people. Often the sponsor will be a member of the project board – but this need not necessarily be the case. The sponsor can be anyone that the project board decides has the ability to support and 'champion', if necessary, the cause of the project and the project manager.

Clearly the sponsor needs to be someone who has the respect of the people involved in the project and ideally should be someone with enough 'clout' or status to be able to support the project manager if needed. The sponsor or champion is a kind of mentor, keeping an eye on things, available to give help and advice if asked, but only intervening if things are clearly going off track. The role of the sponsor is not to be merely an observer. The sponsor has a vital role in the project – but not a hands-on role. The sponsor is there to act on behalf of the project board and in support of the project manager.

The customer/client

The customer is usually the person who wants the problem solved. It is the customer who formally or informally approaches the project board and requests that a certain course of action is taken. Often the customer approaches the project board with both the problem and a solution.

This can be a danger point as the solution may not have been well thought out. Successful project managers are very wary when this scenario occurs. The customer, along with the users, is the ultimate arbiter of the project's success. The customer's role is not an operational role in the project. The customer is responsible for agreeing the 'deliverables' and 'success criteria' at the start of the project.

Sometimes it is not easy to see who the real customer/client is. Suppose you are part of a voluntary group, working with other interested parties, such as the town council, involved in creating a 'Youth Café' in a town – somewhere for young people to meet and relax. Who is the customer – the young people or the town council? And suppose you had some Lottery funding – who is the customer now?

The users

These are the people who will benefit or suffer as a result of the project. Users are not meant to suffer as a result of a project – but they often do. Sometimes this is because the customer/client interprets their needs incorrectly or they are not fully honest about their needs. Successful project managers are aware of this possibility and do all they can to get in touch with the users to verify the real needs. Getting one or two users on the project team is helpful but is not foolproof.

The project manager

The project manager runs the project. The project manager's key tasks are:

- Deciding on the system (procedures) that will be used to run the project.
- Picking the project team.
- Agreeing roles and responsibilities.
- Getting an agreed project definition statement signed off – this will include goals and success criteria, budgets, milestones, etc.
- Delegating tasks to the project team.
- Monitoring the project.
- Reporting progress to the project board.
- Liaising with the sponsor.
- Supporting the project team.
- Closing the project at the end.

Ideally the project manager should not be heavily involved – if at all – in day-to-day project tasks. This is the job of the project team. The project manager's work is to run the project. It is a full-time management role, not an operational one. Also, it is best if the project manager does not have a technical role within the project. It is difficult to be objective and assess priorities in an unbiased way if you are also responsible for delivering a particular component of the project.

The project team

Many people make the point that they are managing a project alone without a team. When asked to reflect on whether this is really the case, they often concede that there is a team, or needs to be a team but they had not analysed the project in that way. They were too busy 'getting on with it'.

In almost every project there is a customer, a deliverable, a project team (even if they are not called that and do not realise they are part of a project), a project manager and a sponsor or champion of the project. The following exercise may help to clarify this point.

 **Example**

A personnel manager asked a member of her staff to introduce user involvement into recruitment and selection within the department wherever possible. He set about his task with some enthusiasm as he was very keen for this to happen and he also liked working on his own. The first problem encountered was that the admin. staff were 'too busy' to give him the information he had requested. He then realised that he did not have the technical knowledge about some of the jobs involved and he did not really know how make the best of the user involvement as he wasn't used to working with users. If when starting on the project he had set up a project group containing the key players, including the users, many of the difficulties would have been avoided including that of status, responsibility and know how.

Understanding the project anatomy

A useful exercise is to draw out a blank set of squares, see Figure 3.1 (page 14), then think about a project you have worked on or are going to work on and put in the names of the people who will fill the various roles. If you have difficulty with this, you might like to reflect on whether the implication is that the project needs to be better thought out.

 **Example**

Sometimes it is possible for a person to appear in more than one square, especially on a small project. In a family wedding, for example, the bride and groom are the customers, but the bride is also part of the project team if she is responsible for choosing her wedding dress. The project manager nearly always is the bride's mother and the project board role is often taken by the bride's father, not getting too muddled in the detail, but watching to see that the overall project is on track – especially the budget! Both may have team responsibilities too – booking cars, caterers, etc. When people have dual roles it is important for that person and others in the project to understand which role the person is in at any given time.

 Example

The UK Government appointed a chairperson for the 'UK Bid for the 2012 Olympic Games'. In one of her first interviews she explained that her immediate task was to appoint a project manager. In effect the chairperson is the sponsor of the project. The Government is the project board and the project manager will report to the Government via the sponsor.

Chapter 4
The Project Manager's Role

The project manager's responsibilities

The project manager should be appointed by the project board when it makes the decision to approve a project. From then on, throughout the life of the project, the project manager has the key role and is responsible to the project board for the smooth running of the project in its entirety.

The project manger is responsible for setting up and running the initial project definition meeting and subsequent reviews, right through to the final project closure and post project review meetings.

Throughout the life of the project they need to ensure that the project team and all other parties to the project are fully briefed and committed to the project.

The project manager is responsible for being very clear about the objectives of the task in hand. In effect they must have a 'video' playing inside their head showing the task or project being done – or 'rolling out' in the required manner. This 'video' is the quality standard that they then try to deliver.

A project manager is responsible for:
- quantity
- quality
- safety
- training
- welfare
- discipline

All these involve people.

The project manager as a role model

Management also includes managing yourself! It is important that the project manager sets a good example to other participants in the project. The project manager should be a role model. Your team will be looking to you for a lead and some of the areas where you need to be beyond reproach include:
- your time management skills
- your people skills
- your behavioural skills
- your technical skills

Project management involves:
- clout
- status
- know how

Clout

Clout is power – the ability to coerce people to do things that they do not wish to do. All line managers have clout. Clout exists because the line manager influences promotion, pay, holidays, perks, who gets the best assignments and who gets the worst jobs. Managers are not meant to manage using clout. Many managers have difficulty with the concept that the use of power is to be avoided. They say that it is perfectly reasonable to order subordinates to do things. True enough – and sometimes it is necessary and perfectly acceptable.

 The more a manager has to use power to get things done the sooner the day will come when productivity will begin to fall away until eventually there will be a strong resistance and a general lack of co-operation.

Sometimes clout works for a manager and the manager does not even realise it. An example might be the following.

Example

A manager (unaware of, or choosing to ignore, the Human Rights Act) announces that all staff must work during the weekend to get a job done. The staff's response is 'when do you want us in?' The manager says 'Come in at 8.00am on Saturday. Have a lie in on Sunday, come in at 8.30 am'. There is no resistance to the manager's plan. The manager thinks that charm and charisma have carried the day. The reality is that the group is aware that appraisal documentation is currently circulating so now is not the best time to protest!

Often project managers have no power or 'clout' as many of the people involved in a project do not report to the project manager in a formal sense. At best they will be seconded to the project, at worst they will be 'borrowed'. Whilst this is undesirable – and to be avoided if possible – it is unfortunately a reality – hence project managers have to motivate and manage people using respect as the major tool.

Status

Some of the people on the project will be senior to the project manager. This is a cause for concern because often the project manager is unable or unwilling to manage them. Some project managers never accept the fact that although certain people may be senior to them within the organisational structure, on the project no one is senior to the project manager, except the project board (and by definition the sponsor) and they do not have a day-to-day role. The project manager must accept the fact that it is part of the remit to manage these senior people when it comes to any matters concerning the project.

Know how

Striving to know more and more about as many disciplines as possible is a wise move. The more knowledgeable you are as a project manager the better. However, most project managers are not experts in all disciplines. (If you are an expert in all disciplines you are to be congratulated and are unlikely to be reading this book!)

The task of managing your experts is potentially fraught with difficulty as you will be unable to refute technical arguments, and you will be less able to know when the wool is being pulled over your eyes.

You will therefore need to take great care in vetting – checking out – the experts that you are considering using on your projects. Past performance and personal recommendations from colleagues are vital in this process. Having, hopefully, selected trustworthy and competent experts you can then manage them using non-technical criteria for the most part i.e. dates, costs and deliverables.

The same applies to the use of volunteers. Many organisations use volunteers and think they could not function (financially) were it not for the volunteers. Volunteers should be selected, trained and be given all relevant information including what is expected of them. They should also be treated as though they were members of staff. In this way you will get the best from your volunteers and they in turn should behave like members of staff – following agreed rules and procedures, e.g. being punctual, following safety procedures and they should be able to do the job appropriately. If they are not up to the task then it should be politely suggested that they should use their skills elsewhere.

If you recruit, or allow yourself to work with, unsuitable people you will spend much of your time undoing or redoing parts of the project in which they were involved. Organisations that rely heavily on volunteers on the basis that 'We couldn't manage without them' should pause and reconsider. Perhaps the truth is you are not managing because of them! The bottom line here is 'Is the person doing a sound job?' If they are then – fine. If they are not, the thinking that must be avoided is 'Well, they are volunteers after all so there is not a lot we can do'. Poor performance cannot be accepted whatever the circumstances.

You only need a few good people to get a good deal of work done.

Profile of a top project manager

To be a world class project manager it is essential to be a well rounded professional with the following skill set:

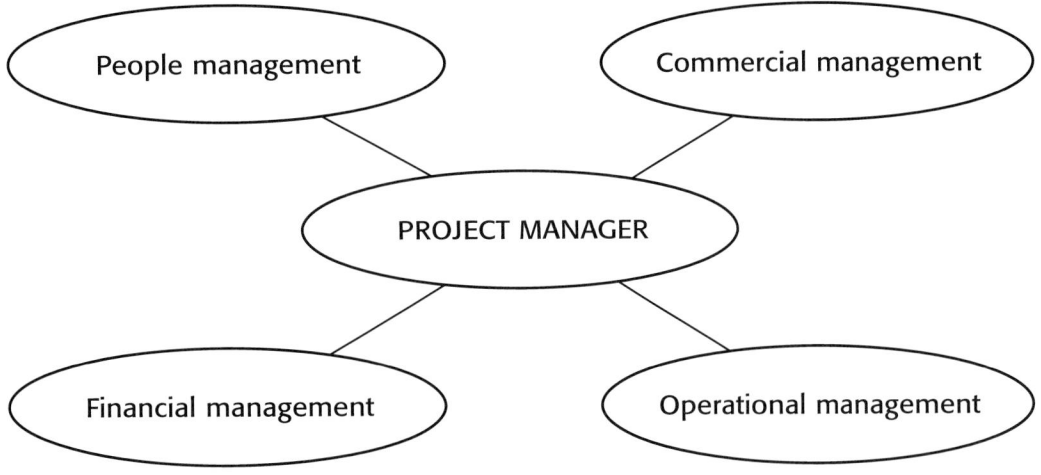

Figure 4.1

People management

Many things influence the success or failure of a project but the key ingredient for success is the people. We have previously mentioned the need for committed people who know what is going on. It is the project manager's responsibility to lead and motivate the project team.

The world's top project managers are all good people managers.

Commercial management

Top project managers are commercially aware. They know the project contract or scope inside out and backwards. They understand the law. They understand how an apparently innocuous action can have massive legal implications if things go wrong. They also know what they don't know; they know when to check before acting. They are always aware when a request is 'outside the scope' of the project and they are meticulous when it comes to 'change management', see Chapter 9.

Financial management

Top project managers are not afraid of the financial aspects of project management. Top project managers do not subscribe to the 'I leave all that figure work to other people' syndrome. They will know how much they have to spend, how the money should be spent, the actual spend and have contingency money available in case of need. They do not usually keep the financial records but will certainly always be aware of the financial situation.

Operational management

Top project managers are good 'at the coalface' – where the work is done. They know the ropes. They have credibility with the rank and file operational staff. They speak the same language and they can pass any test that is set them in the early days of a relationship (tests are always set by subordinates in the early days of a relationship to find out what the person is made of!). As a result they earn the respect of their colleagues and gain their confidence.

What can we learn from the top project managers?

You may not be able to say at this moment that you have the full skill set. As a starting point however pause here to consider your own strengths and weaknesses: see the checklist on the next page.

The skills needed by a project manager

As a project manager, you will need to exercise a high degree of managerial skill in order to motivate and manage the people because it is on their efforts that the project will succeed or fail. See the checklist on page 24.

Strengths and weaknesses checklist

Give yourself a score against each category and make a few notes about your strengths and weaknesses?

Category	Strengths	Weaknesses
People skills		
Commercial skills		
Financial skills		
Operational skills		

Managerial skills – self-assessment checklist

Mark yourself out of ten against each item in the list.	SCORE

- Being a clear, persuasive communicator, able to explain new concepts and ideas.

- Appreciating the importance of careful realistic planning and being able to apply previous experience to benefit from the lessons of past successes and failures.

- Understanding information needed to run a project effectively.

- Being a well-organised and efficient manager, capable of controlling a variety of tasks in parallel and managing conflicting demands on people's time (including your own time).

- Being an effective leader, able to motivate a cross-functional team and encourage the team individually and collectively to make the best possible contribution to the overall project.

- Being proactive and results-oriented; maintaining a clear perspective on priorities and risks and taking nothing for granted.

- Understanding the importance of thoroughness and being able to combine attention to detail with maintaining a strategic and conceptual view of the project.

- Being excellent at analysing and solving problems.

- Having the financial skills needed to apply good commercial judgement in evaluating risk and in assessing value for money. The project manager must also apply appropriate financial control over the project.

- Being able to prepare a business case for any investment required.

- Being literate in the use of appropriate IT tools.

The project manager and the project team

The project manager is responsible for the performance of the project team. It therefore makes sense for the project manager to pick the project team – or at the very least have a high input into the composition of the project team. The project manager must not accept a team that he/she thinks is not up to the challenge of the project. For a project to be successful it is essential to have the appropriate people with the required skills working effectively together as a team for the duration of the project. Sophisticated project management skills and techniques will be of little use if the project team cannot work together successfully.

For any successful team activity it is essential that the team is clear about its objectives. The project manager must ensure that the team is clear about:

- the project goals **and** non-goals
- project organisation
- customers/clients
- solutions
- project plan
- project team working methods
- external influences

The project team will have been assembled and briefed during the project definition stage of the project, and when they have been fully briefed, work can commence.

More information on project team selection and team performance is to be found in Section 3.

Section 2

The Project Management Process

Earlier we identified that a project could be thought of in three stages thus:

- Clarification stage
- Planning stage
- Delivery stage

The clarification or project start-up meeting

The first stage is where we go from identifying the problem or opportunity, to working out, in principle, an agreed solution.

Let us assume that the project board has agreed to go ahead with a project. It could be a major project but might be a mini project, i.e. a feasibility study, to see if a major project is justified. Let us assume that the project board has appointed a project manager. What happens then?

The first thing the project manager should do is set up a meeting where clarification of objectives can take place. This meeting is sometimes called the project definition meeting or project start-up meeting. A suggested agenda for the meeting follows later in this chapter. The clarification stage of the project is the time when all the arguments should take place.

Anticipation being the key to successful project management – look ahead at this time and try to anticipate and raise problems with a view to arguing things through and putting plans in place **now** rather than wait for the problems to occur.

The clarification or project definition stage can take 20 minutes, 20 hours or 20 months – depending on the project complexity.

 The output from this stage – 'the deliverable' – is the project definition report.

All organisations use different terms for this document – but terminology is not important. The **key thing** is that:

- The meeting takes place.
- The above actions are taken, the results are documented.
- The agreement is signed off.

As mentioned before, sign off means that the key players in the project read a copy of the report and show their agreement to it by **signing it**.

In the special needs case study referred to in the foreword, no project definition meeting took place, no agreed actions were documented and there was no sign off. The Head did the thinking for everybody and just got on with things with the minimum of communication. (It was after all a simple relocation exercise!) There was no group involvement and no chance for the group to anticipate problems. Had there been a project definition meeting, many, but not all, of the problems would have been anticipated.

The heated staff meeting that followed the first move became, in effect, the project definition meeting for the second move.

Most large organisations have a formal document for this but in a small organisation it is sufficient to have a memo or one page document that people sign.

 Having documented sign-off will save hours of discussion later in the project.

The signed document is the 'bible' – or contract – for running the rest of the project.

At all review stages of the project this document will form the basis of the review meeting. Any major changes to the project will be dealt with by the change management procedure and the master document will be amended, approved at a review meeting, and signed off. That way any 'moving of the goalposts' – and this **will** happen – will be tracked and the master document will accurately reflect the true nature of the project, including any major changes.

Unless there is a formal document, setting out objectives, success criteria, roles and responsibilities, risk, safety and security, systems and procedures, plans, budgets and project changes, there is no way that the project can be audited or measured. This then means that the project can drift along, and wander off course, being changed and changed again until in the end even people close to the project will be unsure as to where things are headed and why.

The agenda for the clarification meeting

The deliverables from the clarification meeting are:
- The project team is put together.
- The project objectives are revisited and success criteria are clarified.
- Roles and responsibilities are confirmed.
- The system for running the project is agreed – including change control.
- A risk log is developed.
- Safety and security issues are considered.
- A 'broad brush' plan is agreed – main timings and provisional budget.

Let us now consider in more detail each aspect to be dealt with at the clarification meeting:

Putting the project team together

Project team selection is a key aspect of project management, yet it is an area often neglected. For a project to be successful it is essential to have the appropriate people with the required skills working effectively together as a team for the duration of the project. Sophisticated project management skills and techniques will be of little use if the project team cannot work together successfully.

Working together successfully does not mean that there will never be disagreements, even heated discussions, but it does mean that the team will resolve issues and then implement what is agreed.

Most project teams are put together without any thought as to whether or not they are suitable for the job in hand. Some teams are chosen – not chosen would be a better phrase – on the basis that there is a group of people already in existence, i.e. a department or section, and it is automatically assumed that they will manage any project with a title that seems remotely to do with them. This occurs in many in-house projects, where a manager or supervisor is given a project to manage and is expected to use their existing team. No judgement is made as to the suitability of the team for the project in hand. A regular comment is that, often, the project manager has little or no influence on the selection of the project team.

The project manager should pick the project team. Mostly this does not happen but it is vital that the project manager is happy with the team that is selected.

In the case of a small project or a small feasibility study the project manager may decide to proceed alone. This is justifiable in a small number of cases, but bearing in mind that the project manager should not have an operational role this should be the exception not the rule.

Re-visiting the project objectives

All projects involve a balance between three things:

- time
- cost
- performance/quality

Usually this is depicted by a triangle thus.

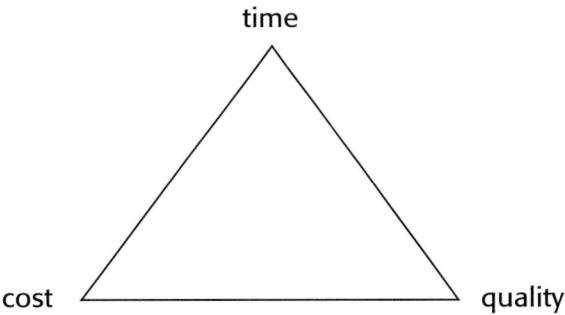

Figure 5.1

At the start of the project it is worthwhile agreeing which of these is the No 1 criterion. For example, if you were developing a pharmaceutical product, then **quality** would be the top priority. Rushing a project such as this or cost cutting is out of the question because no one wants to see another medical disaster. So, if the project begins to run late then extra resources in the form of more people or more hours must be employed. If there is no funding available for this then the launch date for the product must go back. There is no way that quality/performance can be compromised.

On the other hand, if you are locating to new premises and are moving many employees hundreds of miles to the new location, then **timing** is critical as employee's partners need to find employment in the new location and schooling has to be arranged for children. If the refurbishment of the new building starts to run late, additional labour, and hence more money, can be put into the job. If there is no money in the budget then quality will have to be reduced, at least in the short term, and people may have to start work in the new offices before they are fully finished. This will be subject to there being no safety issues of course.

Re-visiting the project objectives is a key area in ensuring the project is properly focussed. Many projects start out with agreed objectives only to find that at the project definition meeting some changes, sometimes major, are agreed.

 Example

A hospital manager in rural Suffolk called in a newly appointed trainee manager one day and asked him to introduce a mini-bus service to bring in staff from outlying villages. The objective given to the trainee manager was 'get a bus service in place asap'. Being new to the organisation and to the role, the trainee did not ask for the reasoning behind the request.

Three months later the hospital was running an efficient but complex and costly bussing system involving several vehicles to transport over 100 employees from around the neighbouring countryside. The trainee was congratulated on a job well done.

About six months later the trainee learned that the logic behind the bussing decision had been reached after a brief discussion at a board meeting. The board was anxious to reduce high labour turnover and absenteeism figures in the organisation and had concluded that the cause was the lack of a decent bus service in the area. The trainee manager had a discreet look at the past and current labour turnover and absenteeism figures. There had been no change.

The objective given to the trainee should have been 'we have a labour turnover and absenteeism problem – find a solution'.

The above is a classic example of poor objective setting resulting from poor problem solving techniques, i.e. tackling the symptom not the real problem. This led to clear, but incorrect, project objectives. The ensuing project was well executed, delivered a well-engineered solution, on time and to budget. At one level, a successful project, but at another level a lost opportunity.

Establishing success criteria

There should be **specific** conditions that exist when an activity or a project has been **successfully completed**. Success criteria are the quality control parameters for any project.

If we consider the scenario above we can see that no success criteria existed or if they did they were to do with the bus service and not with the real problem of absenteeism. Because no success criteria were set, the above project can be seen as a success or a failure depending on which view is taken.

Setting success criteria is essential for every project. It does three things:

- It helps all participants to focus on the issues at the start of a project.
- It ensures that there can be no doubt about whether or not the project is finished.
- It enables the success or failure of the project to be evaluated.

Remember — we have already said that success criteria must be SMART — specific, measurable, achievable and agreed, realistic and timely.

Setting SMART success criteria is not as easy as it sounds. If you set silly success criteria you will encourage silly behaviour.

For example, if the performance of salespeople is measured by the number of calls made in a day they will make a lot of calls. They may not call on the best people and the calls may be brief, even leaving a card at reception may qualify as a call if the pressure for numbers is on.

There was a time when the Government measured school performance largely by examination results. Some schools then only entered young people for examinations whom they thought would pass — thereby ensuring an excellent pass rate.

When fixing project success criteria, it is important to focus on the four or five top level criteria that determine success or failure for the project. Do not get bogged down at this stage with the many, important, but secondary, success criteria that will be present in the project. You are looking at this stage for the four or five measures which, if met, will mean that the secondary measures will in all probability be right too.

 Example

A self-employed consultant has an on-going project called 'running the business'. The success criteria are:

- number of days booked
- number of days worked
- rate per day
- money owed
- new or lost clients

By keeping an eye on these five criteria the business can be easily monitored.

The days worked and days booked figures give a clear indication of the current and likely level of business. This, coupled with the rate per day gives the likely earnings. Keeping the money owed figure at a set (low!) level ensures good cash flow and the new or lost client figure is a good indicator of whether or not you are getting repeat business.

You could measure all sorts of things, typing errors for example. Sending out letters or giving out notes with typing errors in them is something to be avoided in any organisation, but if the new or lost client figure is running at around one per year it is reasonable to assume that the quality of documentation is not causing a problem.

Confirming roles and responsibilities

This is where we confirm the key roles agreed earlier and confirm the project team members and their availability – a key factor. On large projects it is usual for job descriptions to be produced for all of the key players. It is worth doing this, even on smaller projects, it does not take that long and it focuses the mind. Also it can help to avoid confusion later. Unless roles and responsibilities are formally acknowledged and documented, any one can join or leave the project at any time and this can lead to confusion as the following true story shows.

 Example

Julie, a freelance consultant, was commissioned by a local authority to manage a project, the culmination of which was that an information handbook would be issued to all the young people 'in care' in the authority. At the time of the appointment the senior officer of the authority told Julie that within the authority worked someone called Valerie and warned Julie not to involve her in any way with the project. Since the project team had already been set up (verbally) and Julie had already met them all she agreed not to involve Valerie.

Julie then ploughed on with the work, engaged writers, edited the copy, had it checked by the legal department, engaged a printer and held progress meetings. All went well. About four weeks before the launch of the handbook, the team met to finalise details, such as which cartoons to use in the handbook to make it more user-friendly.

As they began their meeting someone entered the room and introduced herself as Valerie. She told them that she was the Publicity Officer for the authority and that any printed documentation issued by the authority was her responsibility! At that point Julie should have been able to refer to the project definition document had it existed, and point out to Valerie that she was not listed as being a player in the project.

Somewhat nonplussed, the group decided to humour Valerie, after all they were so close to the finishing line that even if they tripped now they would still fall over the line, or so they thought! They involved Valerie, gave her a small task to do which she agreed to and off she went, taking with her the project file as she needed to refer to it for information.

She then went missing. No one could find her, or the project file. Julie then heard from the printer. He had been contacted by Valerie and told not to print any handbooks as he would not be paid. Julie contacted her employer at the authority who could not locate Valerie or resolve the situation. Using other sources Julie finally, after several days, located Valerie and recovered the missing project file.

The launch day arrived and Julie's employer, holding aloft a handbook in each hand, announced to the press that 'Every young person in our care is to receive one of these books'. What the press did not know was that there were only two handbooks! Julie had persuaded the printer to print two as a favour to her.

After some considerable time all the problems were resolved, but it is a salutary lesson that being unclear about roles and responsibilities and not having this documented can cause problems.

Agreeing the system

This is the stage where a decision has to be made about the level of control. Items to be considered will include:

- the frequency of reporting
- the amount of documentation
- the type of documentation
- the frequency and format for project review meetings

Much of this will depend on the importance of the project. Most successful organisations categorise their projects using the Pareto principle (see Chapter 12) to determine the 'big hitters', the 'fairly important' and the 'also rans'. Also most large organisations have written guidelines or procedures for running projects. In other words they are trying, as far as is possible, to turn project work into process work. The guidelines usually give an indication of the criteria for deciding the importance of a project based on past experience within the organisation. Having categorised the project it is then possible, using any guidelines that exist, to determine the level of control that is appropriate for the project.

The Class A projects are the ones that will have the biggest impact on the organisation and will, in most organisations, be run by the book i.e., they will be subjected to all the controls listed in the organisation's procedures. There will be no exceptions. I call them 'Bells and Whistles' projects. Usually the Class A projects are the ones with the biggest budgets but there can be exceptions. A redundancy programme may not necessarily involve a large budget but if the project is badly handled the adverse publicity could be very damaging and demoralising for staff.

For Class B projects there is usually some watering down of the controls and procedures that are required. Often the project manager has the authority to decide the level of control for Class B projects. This allows the project manager to impose Class A controls if they think it is appropriate or even Class C controls. The project manager chooses the appropriate level, usually somewhere between the two. It is important to ensure that the work done to control the project does not detract from actually doing the work on the project. We do not want to be 'using a sledgehammer to crack a nut'.

Class C projects are the many (about 80%) small projects that are done in any organisation. They are important but they are not 'big hitters'. If a Class C project goes wrong the impact on the organisation as a whole will hardly be noticed. These are 'back of an envelope' projects because they can often be controlled and managed by making a few notes.

However, even these projects require clear objectives, success criteria, planning and control or they will go awry. Even something such as organising a skittle evening at the local pub can go awfully wrong if a few controls are not in place. These might be:

- Having a written list of who is going.

- Having written confirmation from the pub.

- Ensuring you have commitment or 'sign off' from the participants by collecting the money in advance!

There is no better way than asking someone to sign a document or pay you some money to find out whether or not they are serious about something.

Change control methods

One of the key items to be agreed at this stage is the question of change control – how changes are to be highlighted, documented and dealt with.

If your organisation has formal procedures there will be instructions as to how to manage changes. However, in most projects change management is an issue that is overlooked, often because people do not wish to accept that changes will occur. Do not allow this to happen. Have the argument now. Even if there is no formal system, changes can be recorded easily by fax, memo or email. Make sure that every one knows that changes **are** going to be managed.

Without change control there is no project control. In Chapter 9 change control is explained in more detail.

Developing a risk log

Here, with all the team present, we put together the first risk log. The risk log is where we record any risks that might threaten the project. It is the start of the Risk Management process that will stay with us throughout the life of the project. Risk management is dealt with more fully in Chapter 8.

Considering safety and security

By safety we mean safety in the health and safety context. Remember some of these issues may have been highlighted when compiling the risk log, but this is a safety net.

Do not fall into the trap of thinking that there is no safety aspect to your project just because it is not an industrial, or construction project. It is not necessary to be building a bridge or a dam to have real safety issues. A weekend away camping with young people is an example that comes to mind. Who does not remember the adventure holiday a few years ago when many young people were tragically drowned whilst out canoeing? Also, what about care workers travelling alone to and from meetings – with someone who has a history of violence in the car? And when you are responsible for booking accommodation for a group of older people, do you check out the fire safety aspects of the hotel?

Sometimes there will be security aspects to be considered in a project. Access to information is a good example. In most organisations access to certain information is restricted. However it is easy to be complacent about information, especially after a project is completed. Personal data about families being used without permission or confidential files that are used and then not replaced in their correct secure position when they are no longer required for the project are two examples.

Developing a broad brush plan

Here we put together a plan showing the big moment or milestones in the project, that is, a broad brush plan with not too much detail. Also at this stage we should start to consider costs and the way they will build up – or if we have a fixed sum to work within we should consider how this will be allocated to the various activities in the project. The broad-brush plan for this book, say, looks like this:

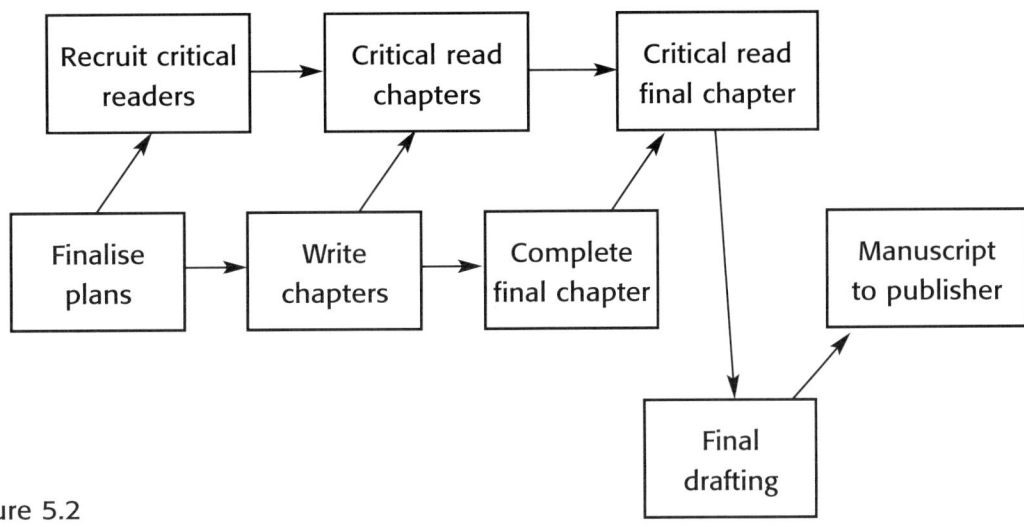

Figure 5.2

All the above activities will need the involvement of all the key players.

Do not fall into the trap of thinking that Player A or Player B does not need to be involved in this or that aspect of the project. At this stage everyone needs to be involved. If you start leaving people out at this stage they will quickly become downhearted and thereafter you will have a major job on your hands to get them to buy in to the project again.

In addition to involving the key players, it is very important to remember the users.

You may have already tried to cover this aspect by getting users co-opted onto the project team, but if this is not the case the users' views must be sought **now**. If this is not done now, the whole project is potentially flawed. The best case scenario is that user information will be discovered later, but not too late for amendments to be made to the project, but at a cost and invariably causing a delay. The worst case scenario is that the project will run its course, meet its criteria, only to be rejected when presented to the users. Involving the users gives the best chance of getting to the real problem behind a project and hence the best chance of lasting success.

 Example

An academic was asked to be a critical reader of some training material aimed at 'Young People in Care'. During the conversation she offered to recommend some young people to act as critical readers too. This offer was turned down not because they already had young people as critical readers but because there was no intention of involving any young people (the ultimate users) in the project.

When all the above activities are completed the project definition report can be finalised.

The project definition report

The project definition report can be a one or two page document or, if you are engaged in a major project it can be a tome. However, in either case, the summary pages, it might be called the 'Top Sheet' should be similar and should show or refer to the information in Figure 5.3 opposite.

The top sheet should always state the objective, on half a page only. This is a well tried and tested principle. If you cannot state your objectives on half a page then, in all probability, you are not clear about your objectives.

Along with your objectives will come your success criteria or deliverables? Remember – top level criteria only and these are bound to include:
- time
- money
- quality – meaning performance.

Figure 5.3: The project definition top sheet

Objective:
State this on half a page only - to include Success Criteria – ideally no more than five – three being:
- Time
- Cost
- Quality   eg
            Specifications
            Performance

Then list or refer to:
- Key Roles and Key Players
- System and Procedures
- Risk, Safety and/or Security
- Change Control

Sign Off

NAME	NAME	NAME	NAME	NAME	NAME

 Sign Off is VITAL for successful project management.

By listing your key success criteria in this way you ensure that the project is not loosely defined. Statements of objectives alone without success criteria as shown above can be open to misinterpretation.

To help you establish these criteria consider the following:

- What are the overall objectives of the project?

- What will be the overall size of the proposed project, and what areas/work will it cover?

- What will be the project deliverables and/or desired outcomes – these will be any key products or end results that the project will deliver (e.g. a new computer system, or policy guidance etc.).

- Exclusions – sometimes it is important to specify what is not going to be covered by the project.

- Constraints – are there any limitations which may impact on the project, for example, in terms of cost, time-scale or quality?

- Interfaces – are there any relationships with any other agencies, projects, business systems and/or procedures that should be mentioned?

- Are there any shared resources that need to be considered?

The other items shown in the diagram can be attached as appendices – but must be addressed and cross-referenced on the top sheet.

In summary, all projects and assignments should have a written project definition statement addressing:

- roles and responsibilities
- success criteria and deliverables
- time
- cost
- performance
- reporting structure
- risk
- safety and security
- change control

This is the 'contract' for the project (sometimes referred to as the 'scope' of the project).

It should be documented, circulated, and **signed off** by the key players and by the project board.

Remember – **No sign off – No project.**

Chapter 6
The Planning Stage: Timings and Critical Activities

The importance of planning

Planning is vital to ensure that everyone involved in the project has information on:

- what is required
- why it is required
- how it will be achieved
- who will achieve it
- when it will be achieved

Planning is about understanding, in detail, what is required and how exactly it will be delivered. Planning is about anticipation. It is about saying 'what if?' Planning is about considering the risks to the project (see Chapter 8). The more you anticipate the things that may catch you out the better prepared you will be to deal with them. When planning, it is worthwhile wearing your black hat, i.e. adopt a pessimistic, worst case scenario, approach, for much of the time. Do not fall into the 'it will be alright on the night' trap. It will not be alright unless you worry about the detail.

Colleagues may tell you that you are worrying too much. It is possible to over-plan but if in doubt err on the side of over-planning. Lack of planning is a characteristic of most unsuccessful projects. The projects are usually very exciting, or chaotic, and highly stressful as various un-anticipated difficulties are encountered – then dealt with 'on the hoof' which usually sends costs sky high as labour and other resources are 'thrown at the problem'.

Most people under-plan. This is because instinctively they know that without a plan they cannot be held to account.

The time spent doing detailed planning will be rewarded when problems arise during the life of the project. However well you plan there will still be things that are overlooked during the planning stage and things that do not go as planned during the project but the fact that you have done a lot of planning will reduce these occurrences to a minimum. Also you will be better prepared to work out the best solution to any difficulties that arise.

Remember that **planning is an on-going process throughout the life of any project.**

- The plan is there to support the project: do not let the plan become the project.
- When the plan needs changing – change it.
- The more pre-planning you do – the less planning changes you will make.

The planning stage

Having produced our project definition report for the project we now know:
- how it is to be controlled
- who is responsible for the key jobs
- the people to be involved
- the reporting procedures
- the preferred timescale

Now we can move on to more detailed planning. The end product of this stage is an agreed plan. When at the planning stage the two main considerations are, how to carry out this stage, and what planning and control methods will be needed for your project?

How to carry out the planning stage

You have two main options:
- Work alone to develop the plan.
- Involve others to develop the plan.

Advantages in working alone:
- quicker
- easier
- no conflict
- no interference
- you get what you want

The biggest problem with doing the planning alone comes when you try to sell the plan to the other members of the team and to other interested parties. Do not be surprised if you get serious opposition.

Advantages of working with others to develop the plan:
- Two or three heads are better than one.
- The plan becomes everyone's plan i.e. Having helped to develop it, the participants are more committed to it.

Any oversight or error in the plan is everyone's responsibility, not just the project manager's, so the steps needed to recover from the situation are more likely to have everyone's support.

 Whilst it is everyone's responsibility, the project manager is accountable.

As with most key stages in project management, planning is best done with all the interested parties present – time-consuming, yes, expensive only in the short term and difficult to control but definitely worth it. Experienced project managers will tell you that it is worth taking extra time at this stage to involve the appropriate people in developing the plan.

What sort of plan do we need?

The plans that you need for a project are determined by the size, complexity and importance of the project. The importance of the project is decided by the project board.

Planning tools

The main tools for project planning are:

- work breakdown structures (WBSs)
- work-to lists
- milestone charts
- bar charts
- resource plans
- network diagrams
- the budget – see Chapter 7

The planning tools and how to use them

Here we will review the techniques starting with network analysis as this is one of the most useful of all planning tools.

Network analysis

Network analysis looks and sounds complicated but appearances are deceptive. Coming to terms with network diagrams is like getting used to the London Underground map, rather off-putting when first seen, but extremely useful, some would say invaluable, once understood. In the same way that the Underground map tells you all you need to know to navigate your way around the Underground system, a network diagram contains most of the information you need to know to navigate your way through a project or assignment.

Figure 6.1 is an example of a network diagram.

Network diagrams show all the activities in a project and the dependencies – i.e., the way they are linked together, meaning which activities need to be completed before other activities can start. They also show timings for the activities and most importantly, they show the 'critical path' – i.e. the path that is controlling the timing of the project.

Drawing a network diagram

The first stage in project planning is to draw what is called a broad-brush plan. This is a plan, or network diagram, showing the large parts of the project and how they link together. At this stage avoid getting into too much detail. Get your team together and any other people who are affected by the project or anyone you think may be able to contribute. You are now ready to plan the project.

Figure 6.1: Network for building a home

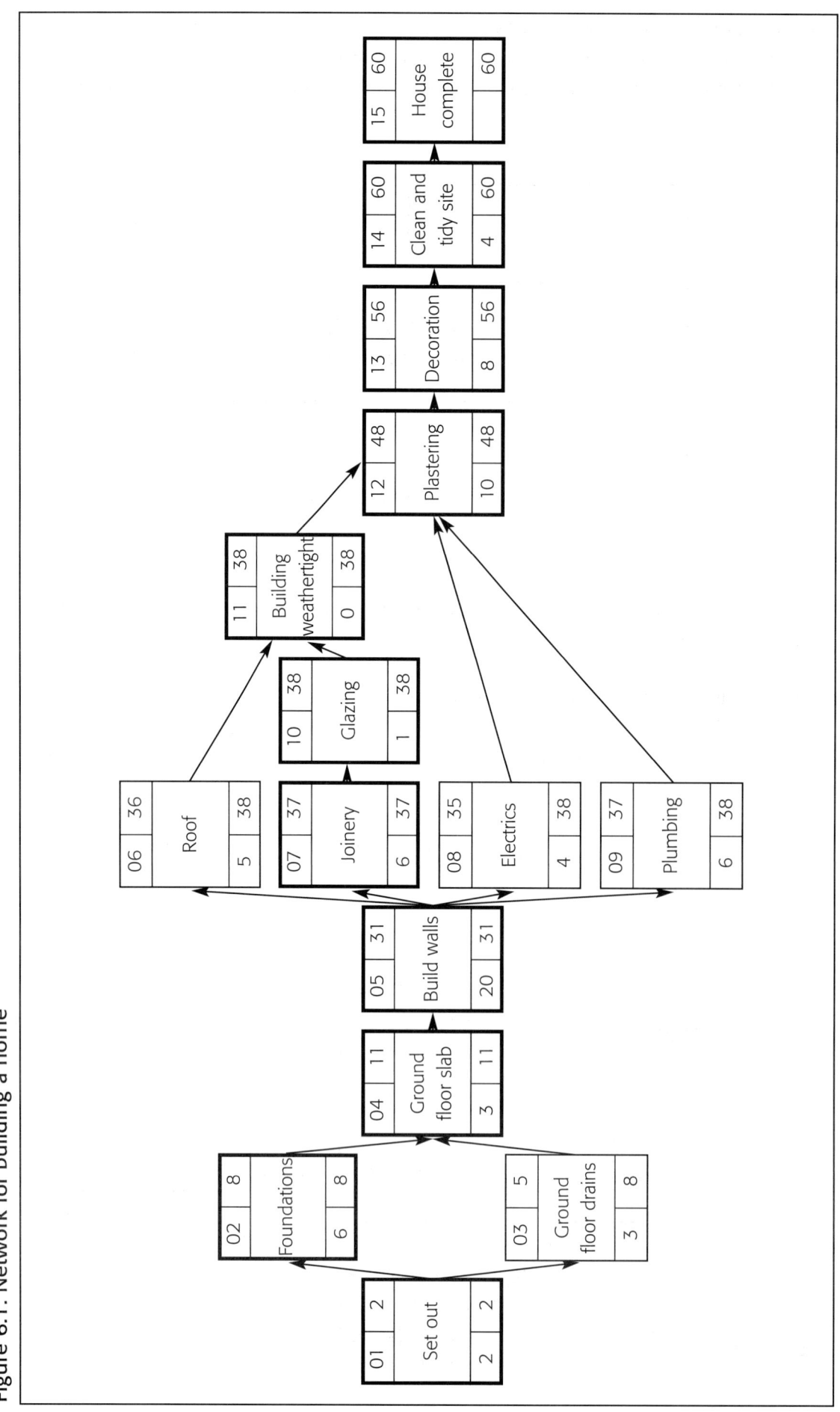

44

Get the group to consider all the activities that must be carried out. Invite each member of the group to write their activities on 'Post -It' notes. Also invite them to consider any activity that will hold them up and get them to make a 'note' for it. The notes should look like this:

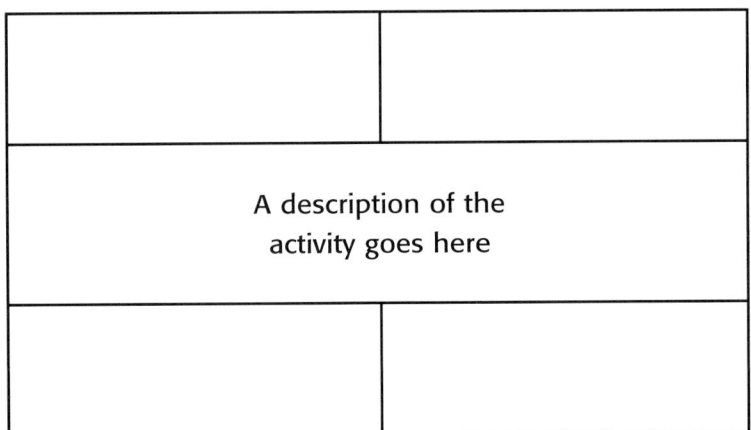

When this is done put all the notes onto a board or a wall and then begin to construct a network as follows.

Take any activity – there is no need to begin at the beginning of the project, you can start anywhere. Place the activity on the wall. Now ask the group to tell you which other activities follow or precede the activity. Place these on the wall and draw arrows, or use other 'Post it' notes as arrows, to show the dependencies.

If, for example, we were producing a network for 'making a cake' it would look something like this:

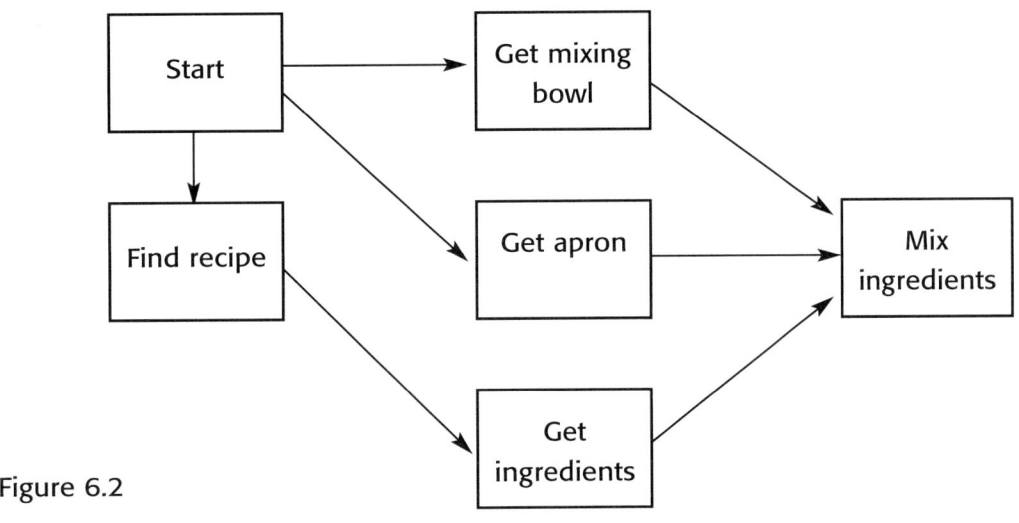

Figure 6.2

At this stage we are considering the logic only – the dependencies. We are not considering any resource limitations. Clearly, if only one person was making the cake, all the activities would be consecutive. This is a very important point. There is often a great desire at this stage to get the plan finished, but it is vital to concentrate on understanding the dependencies. The planning will be sorted out next and will be more likely to be correct if the logic is understood.

Continue with this process until all the notes are on the wall. Make sure that all have a 'predecessor', except the 'start' box, and a successor, except the 'finish' box.

Project network exercise

Draw a network diagram for the following project:

A voluntary organisation has drawn up the following schedule of activities for creating and testing a new website:

Activity	Preceding activity	Duration (weeks)
A	-	2
B	A	2
C	A	4
D	A	3
E	C	3
F	E,B,D	5

This is how it might begin:

'A ' has no preceding activity so it can start whenever you decide to start the project. We can show 'A' thus:

B' can start when 'A' is finished so we can now add 'B' thus:

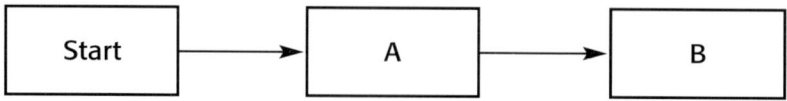

'C' can also start when 'A' is finished so that can be added too:

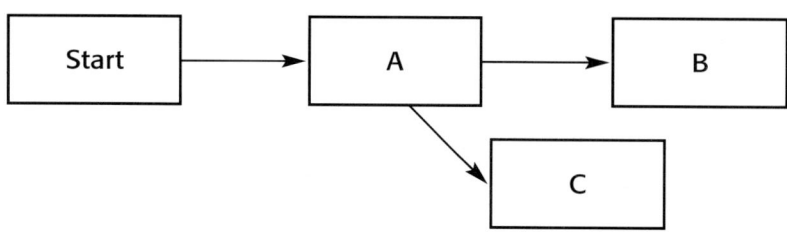

It should now be possible to finish it off. If you are not sure look ahead to Figure 6.3. Your diagram should be the same but without the numbers.

Having drawn the network, we can examine it to satisfy ourselves that it is correct. Any changes to the logic can be made until we are sure that the diagram is a true picture of the way the project goes together.

Be clear that, later in the project, you will almost certainly change the network. Also, later in the project, you may discover that some of the dependencies were wrong or had been misunderstood. This is normal but it does not invalidate the work you have done. By drawing the network and thinking through the logic you will have gained a great understanding of your project which will prove invaluable as the project later unfolds.

Having sorted out the logic we can now address timings. Ask the appropriate person to give you an estimate of the time for each of the activities. Write these on the bottom left hand corner of the 'notes'. Having done this your project plan will look similar to Figure 6.3.

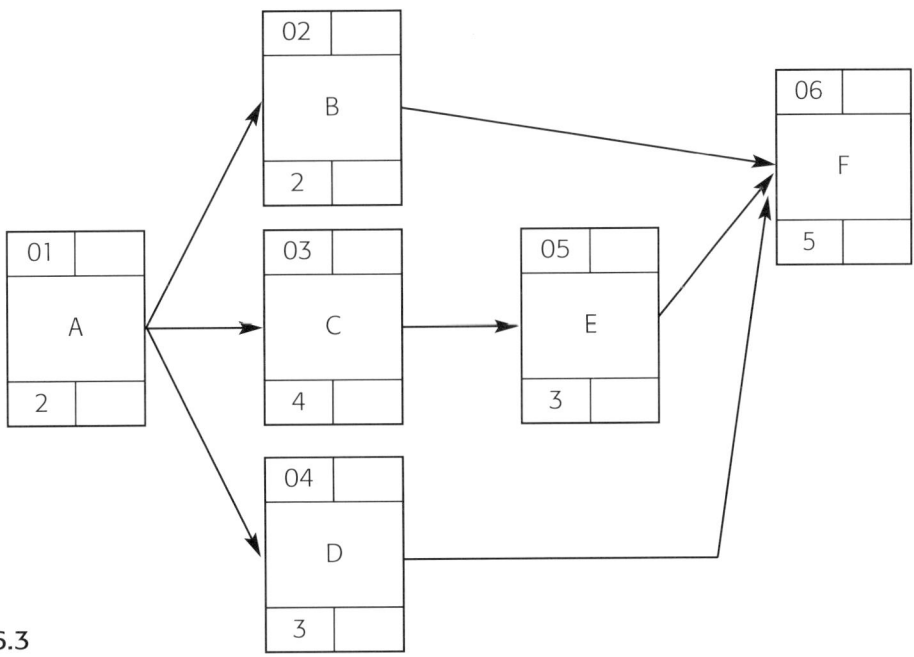

Figure 6.3

The numbers in the top left corners of the boxes are there to identify each box or activity. On a small network such as this they are hardly necessary but on a large network they can be helpful.

The numbers in the bottom left hand corners are the duration times taken from the question. Remember, in a real situation you have to get the timings from the participants in the project.

 As this is an exercise the activities are designated as 'A' and 'B' etc. but in real life always write a description of the activity in the box, never use letters.

Timings

If we assume that we start the project at time zero then the earliest finish time (EFT) for activity 'A' is week 2. Insert this in the top right of the box. If when 'A' is completed we now do activity 'B' then the earliest finish time (EFT) will be week 4. Continue in this manner to complete the network.

The box most likely to give a problem is the final one, activity 'F'. There appear to be three possible answers but a closer examination will show that 'F' cannot start until all the preceding activities are completed. The last one to finish will be 'E', finishing in week 9. So 'F's 'earliest finish' will be 9+5 i.e. week 14.

We now repeat the process but this time we work backwards to establish the latest finish time (LFT). Let us assume that we want this project completed as soon as possible, i.e. by week 14. We put 14 in the bottom right hand square showing this as our latest finish time (LFT) for the project. Activity 'F' takes 5 weeks so it must start at week 9. Therefore any preceding activities must be completed by week 9. This means the latest finish for 'E' and 'B' and 'D' must be week 9. Put this in the bottom right hand corner of the appropriate boxes. Then continue working backwards until you get back to the start box. Here again it may seem that there are three options, but if activity 'A' is allowed to finish later than week 2 it will hold up activity 'C' and 'E' and hence delay the project. The completed network should look like this:

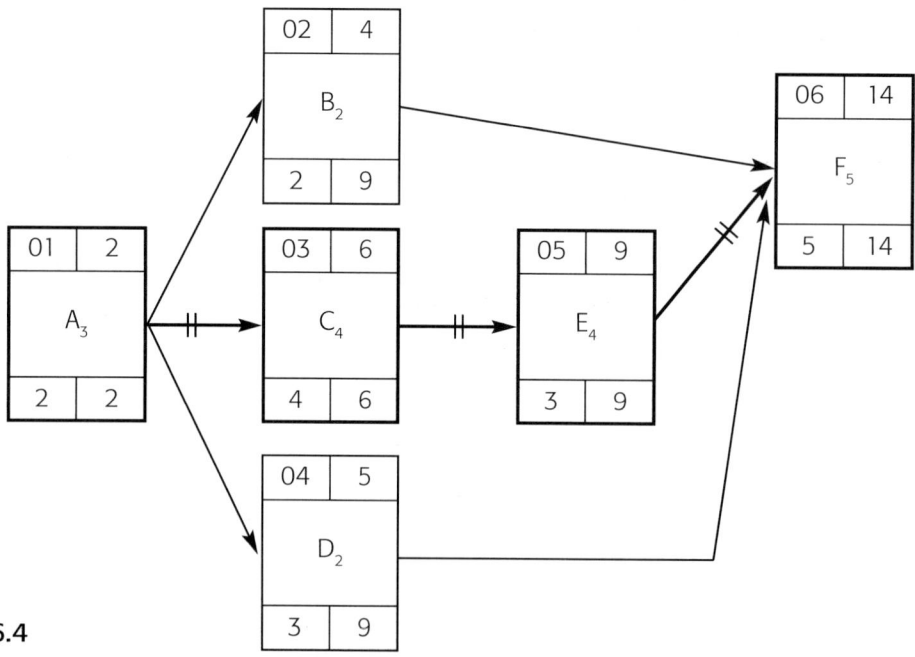

Figure 6.4

We can now see that some of the activities have the same earliest and latest finish. In other words there is no leeway. These activities are 'critical' and are the longest path through the network.

 The *longest* path through the network determines the *shortest* time for project completion.

This is called the 'critical path'. By establishing the critical path we identify the activities that we must complete on time in order to complete the project on time. These are the activities to which we must give priority. Also, if we need to reduce the time for delivering the project these will be the activities on which we will have to make savings.

All networks have a critical path. Some networks have more than one critical path. During the life of a project the critical path may change. This is normal. The key thing is to know where the critical path is so that, as project manager, emphasis can be given to the appropriate activities.

The network we have been working on is quite small and is simple. Larger networks are just larger, they are still as simple. If you can draw and understand a small network you are capable of drawing and understanding large networks. Many people say that if a project has less than 30 activities it is not worth drawing a network but it takes so little time to draw a small network that makes sense to draw one.

The benefits of understanding the logic of a project before doing the planning cannot be overstated. Having produced a broad-brush network for a project you may later need to do another more detailed network, especially if you are working on a major project. The process is exactly the same, just more of it! Follow exactly the same process.

When network planning, think of the wall or white board as a car park, and imagine that it is marked out horizontally in strips. Allocate a strip to each major discipline in the project and keep all the boxes for the discipline within the strip as shown:

Figure 6.5

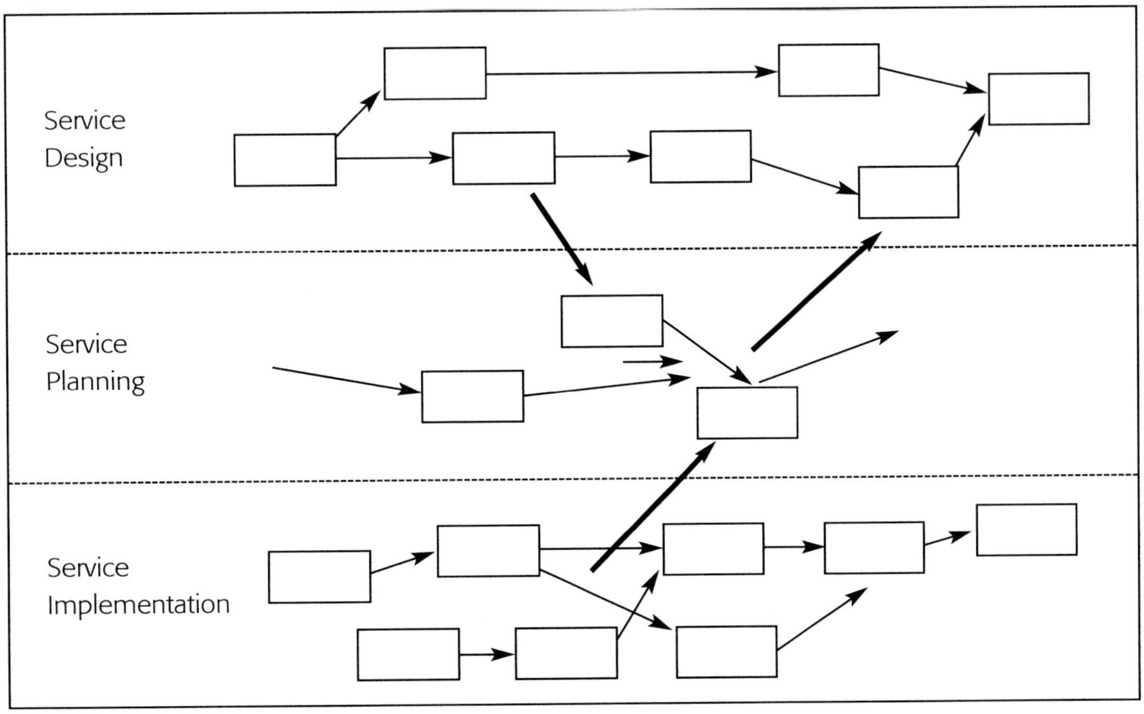

It is then easy for staff working in any one discipline to see its activities in a neat horizontal row but equally easy to see how those activities affect other disciplines.

In the same way it is possible to join separate whole projects together. Suppose you are a publisher working on three books as shown:

Figure 6.6

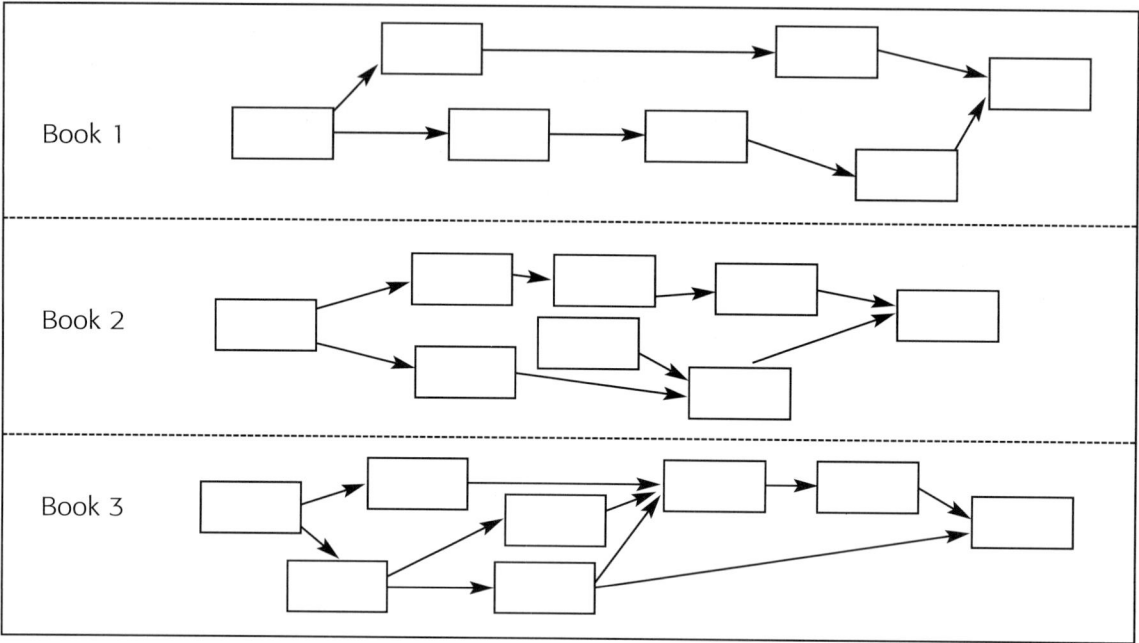

You realise how they each impact upon each other – perhaps a particular activity involves a specialist team of people, say, typesetters, or involves the use of a special piece of equipment that cannot be duplicated. Or perhaps there is a particular resource, printing or proofreading that must be available. If you think the project timings are such that lateness in one project might delay other projects you can join the projects together thus making them one big project, shown:

Figure 6.7

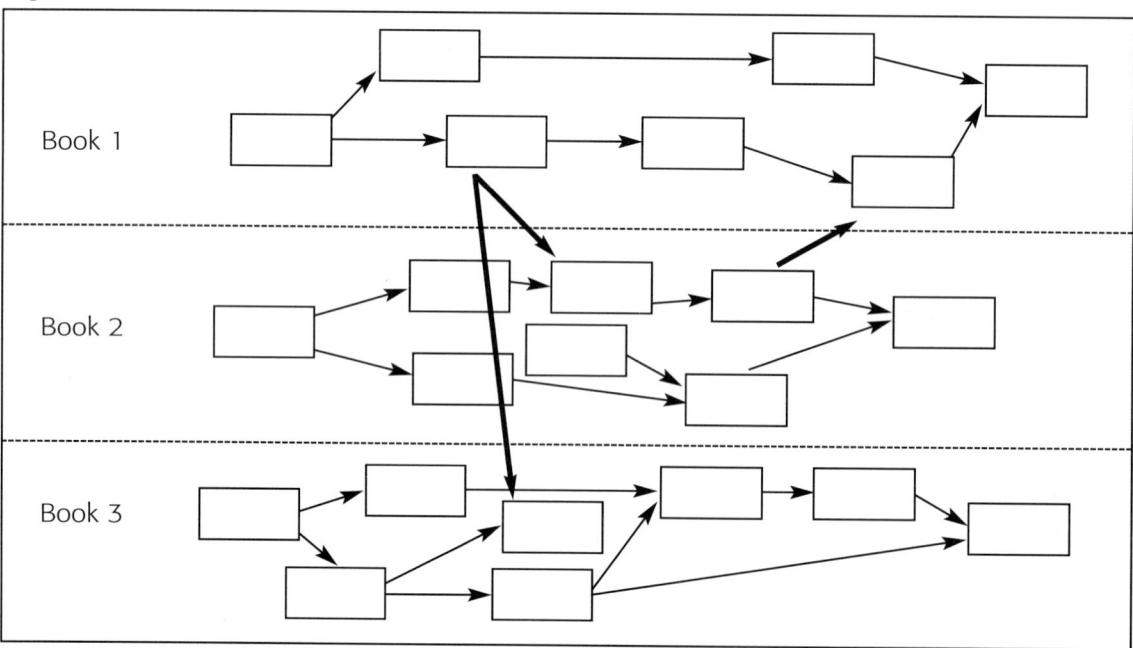

If Book 1 is delayed it will then immediately be necessary to re-schedule the appropriate activities in the other two projects. Once you have completed your network it is important to plan the project. A bar chart is useful for this task.

Bar charts

Bar charts, also called Gantt charts, are charts showing activities (jobs) as a horizontal line or bar drawn to scale on a chart. Activities are listed on the vertical axis. A timescale runs along the horizontal axis. Each activity is shown as a horizontal bar, drawn to scale and starting at its start date and finishing at its finish date. Bar charts are widely used, easy to follow and hence very popular as a project planning and control tool. Often they are the only planning and control tool used – especially on small projects. They are easy for most people to understand and if properly constructed, not too difficult to update.

Simple bar charts such as the one on page 55 have the disadvantage that they do not show dependencies. However, by using a network, or logic diagram, it is possible to incorporate dependencies as shown in the worked example later in the chapter.

Drawing Bar charts

First draw your 'X' and 'Y' axis, then add an appropriate scale.

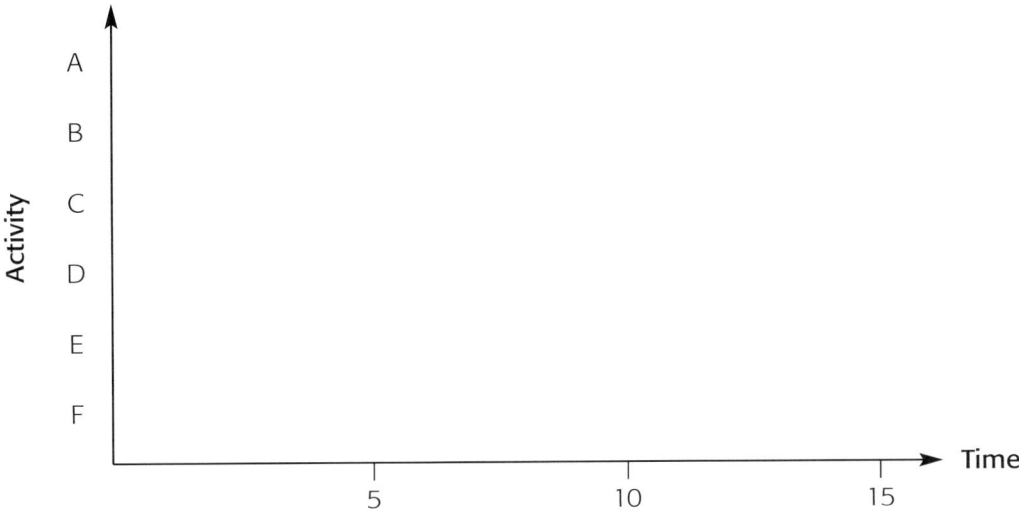

Now consider the activities – firstly 'A' from our earlier example. When is the earliest 'A' can start? – Time zero. Plot this on the chart opposite 'A'. When is the earliest 'A' can finish? – 2 weeks. When is the *latest* 'A' can finish? – Also 2 weeks because 'A' is a critical activity and therefore has no float. Plot this and join the two lines, thus:

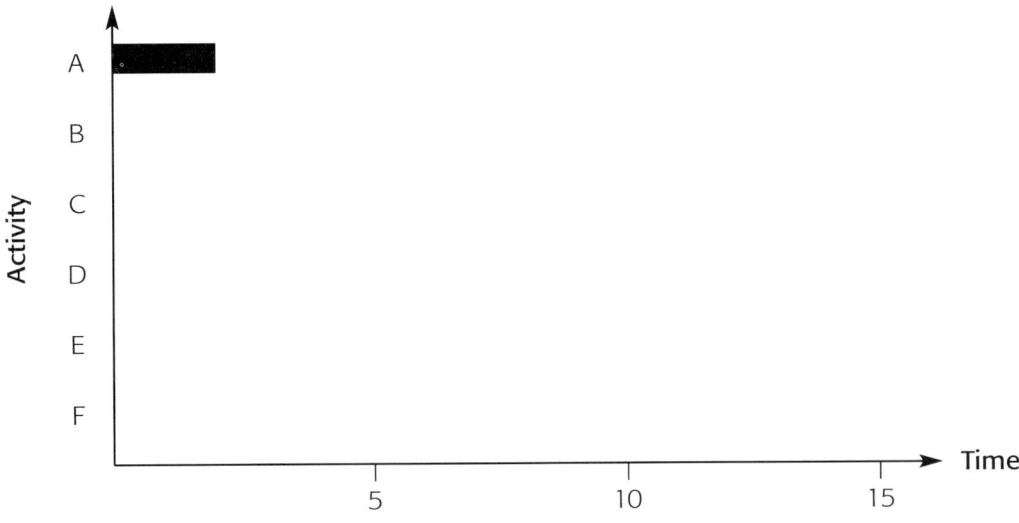

Repeat this process for 'B'

You should get an earliest start of 2 weeks, an earliest finish of 4 weeks and a latest finish of 9 weeks – 'B' can finish as late as week 9 without delaying 'F'. Activity 'B' has 5 weeks float. Plot the points, join the first two points with a firm line and continue with a dotted line to point three:

Your diagram should now look this:

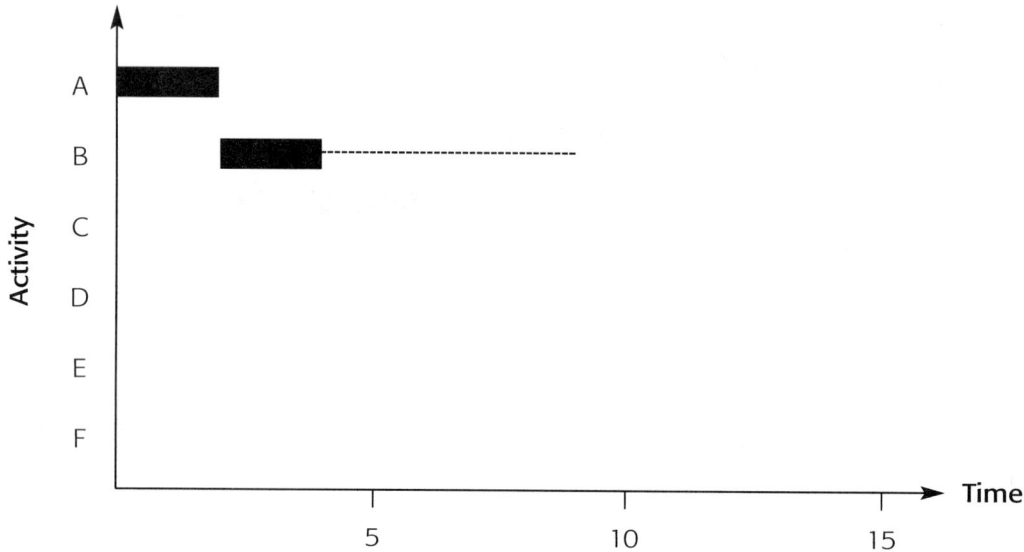

Complete the bar chart yourself for C, D, E and F activities. The answer should be as shown:

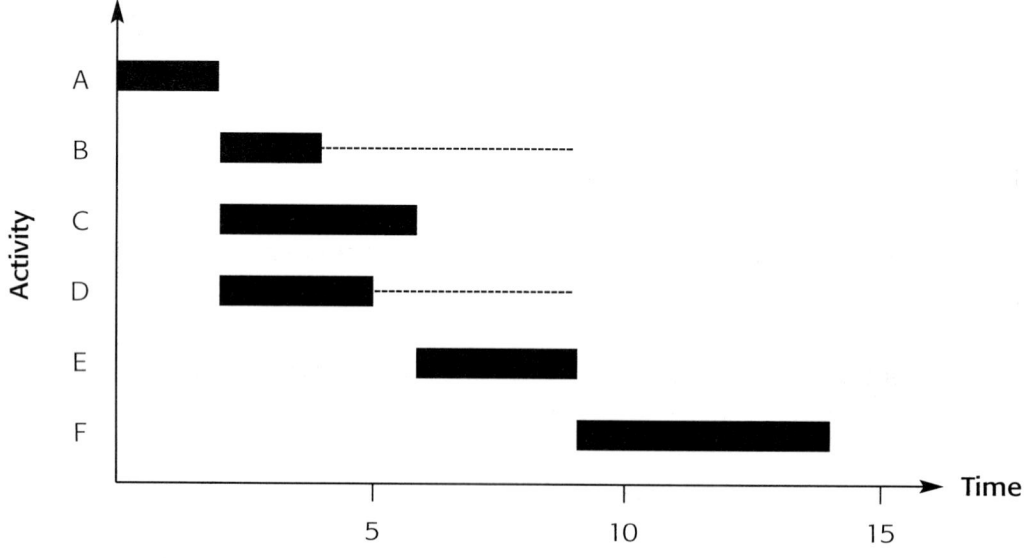

We now need to add the dependency lines. We know that 'B' 'C' and 'D' depend on 'A' so we draw in a vertical line to connect the end of 'A' with the beginning of 'B' 'C' and 'D'. We also know that 'F' depends on 'E' 'C' and 'D; so we draw a vertical line connecting the start of 'F' with the end of 'E' 'C' and 'D. 'B' can be finished by week 4 but need not be finished until week 6. It has 2 weeks float which we show as a dotted line. Similarly 'D' has float. The activities with no dotted lines that have no float are the critical activities

Our finished diagram should now look like this:

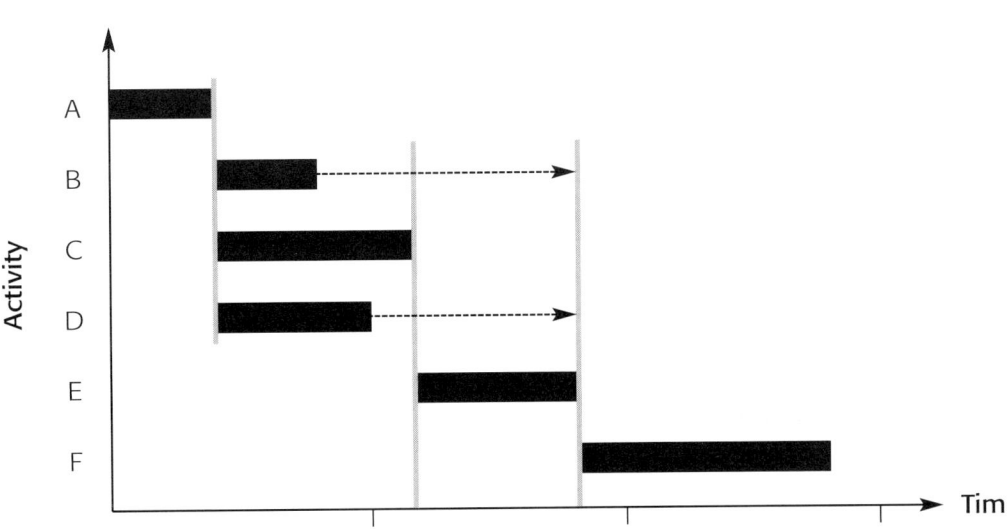

The bar chart shows exactly the same information as the network we drew earlier – but many people feel that bar charts are easier to understand. The project manager must choose the appropriate method for displaying information.

The bar chart clearly shows the dependencies and the float and we can now see all our planning or scheduling options. We can then decide when to start activity 'B' and 'D' bearing in mind that they both have floated.

Before we do, however, we should consider resources in case a resource constraint affects our plan.

Resource plans and histograms

Resource plans are necessary where resources are limited or where multiple projects are running and all are calling on one pool of resources.

Resource plans show, often in histogram form, demand on a particular resource at any time. Resource plans are derived from the bar charts.

A resource histogram is shown in Figure 6.8.

At the top of the diagram is the bar chart and below is the histogram of resources needed. This method is ideal when there is only one resource type such as all youth workers or all carers.

When there are several different disciplines that need resource managing it is better to show resource demand using numbers added to the bar chart as shown in the worked example later in this chapter - see pages 64 to 73.

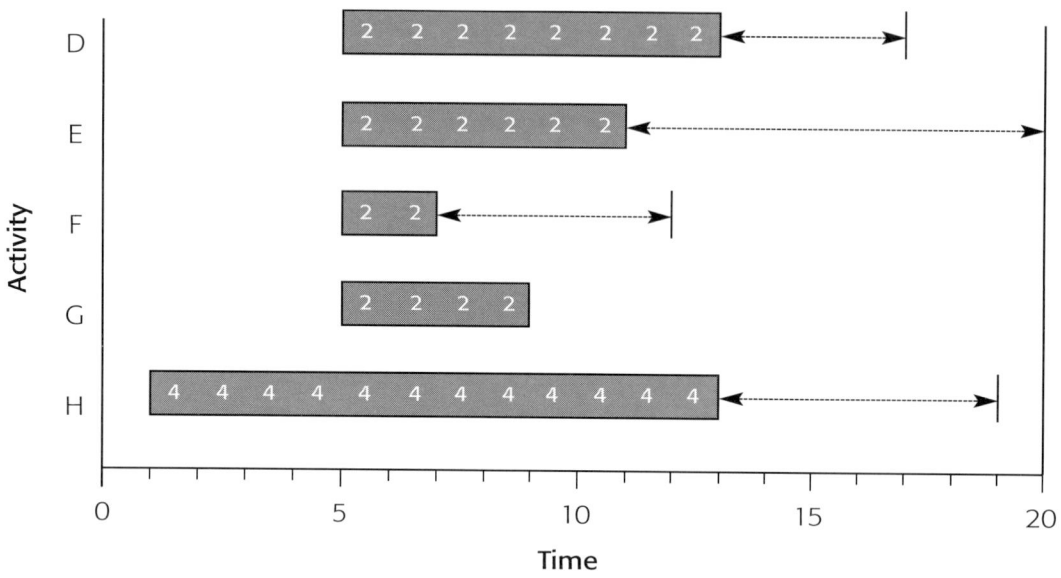

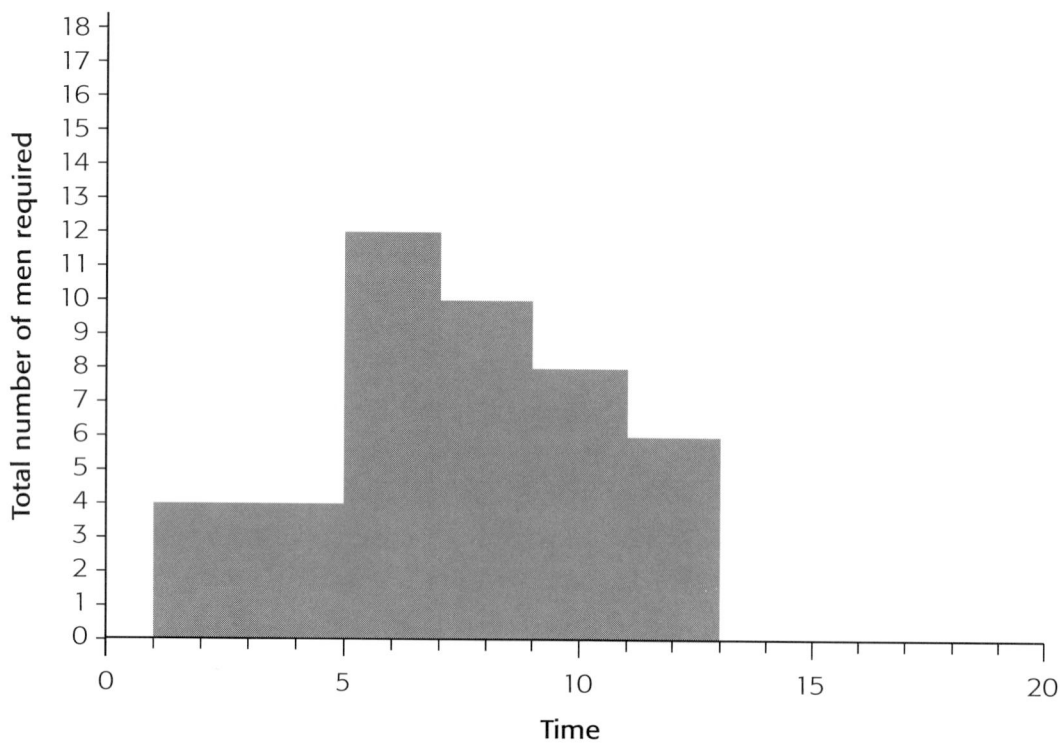

Figure 6.8: A bar chart showing resource requirements with resource histogram below

Suppose all the activities in the plan below (see Figure 6.9) involve care staff. The care staff numbers can be added to the bar chart and then a resource histogram drawn.

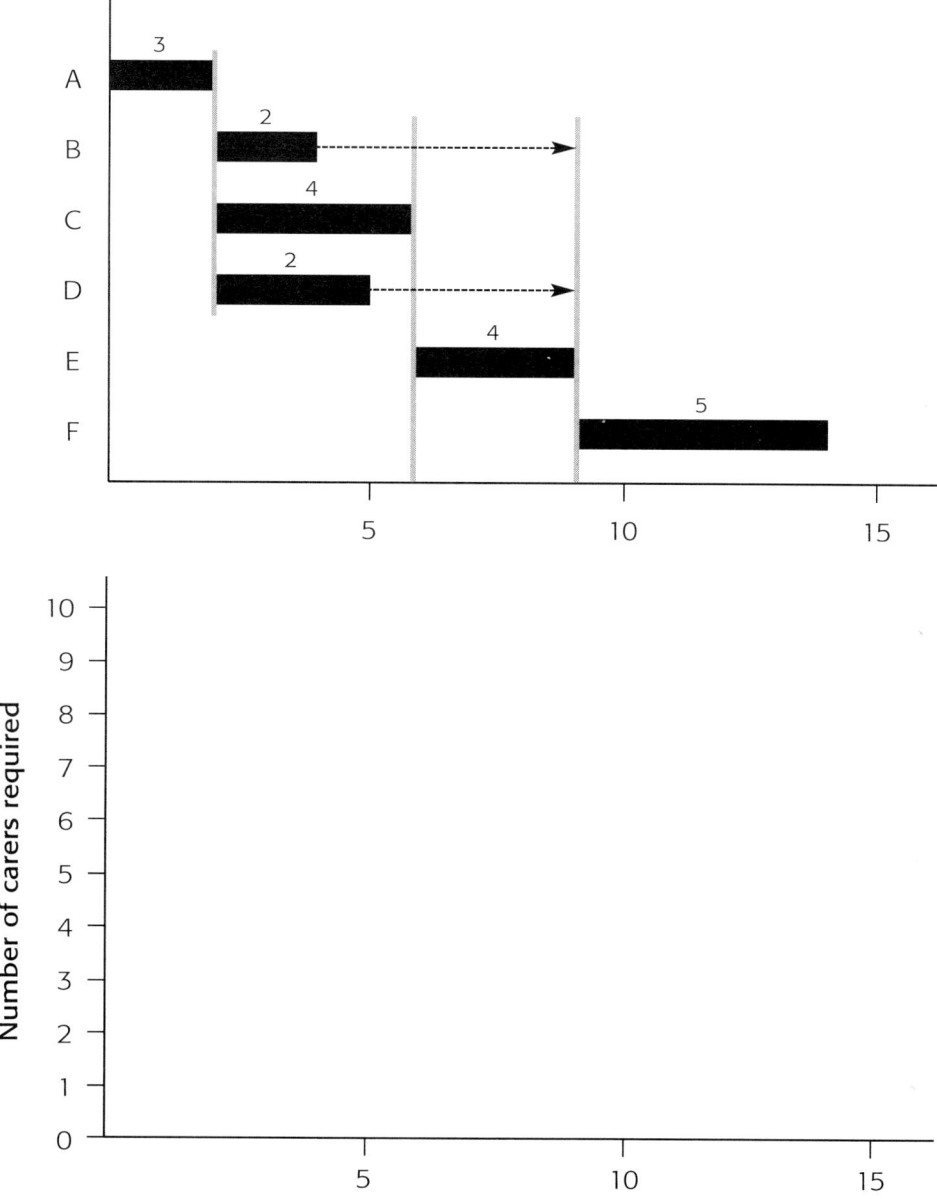

Figure 6.9

At the start of the project, assuming we work to the plan as shown in the bar chart, we will need three care staff for the first two weeks. We then plot this on the histogram.

How many care staff do we need at the start of week 2? And how long do we need them for? Answer – eight are needed from week 2 until week 4 when task 'B' finishes.

Plot this onto the histogram and then work out the remaining requirements. Your finished answer will look like Figure 6.10.

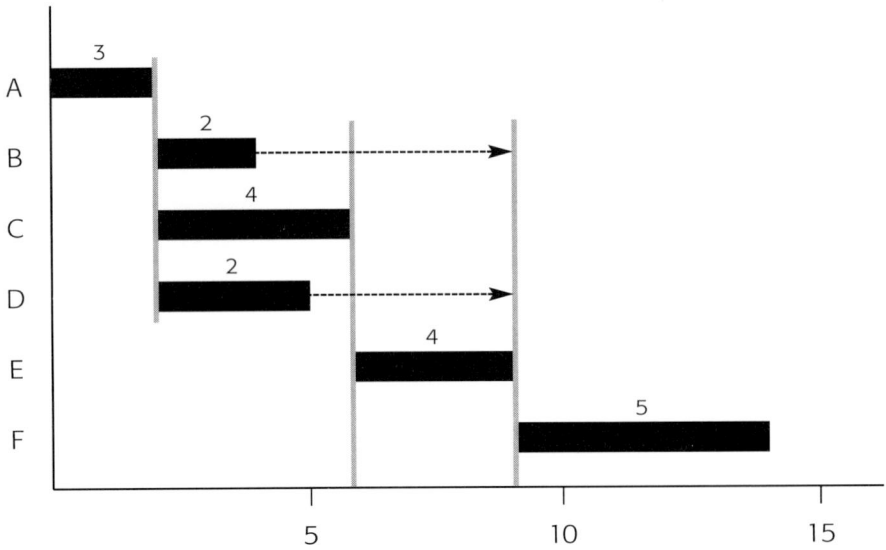

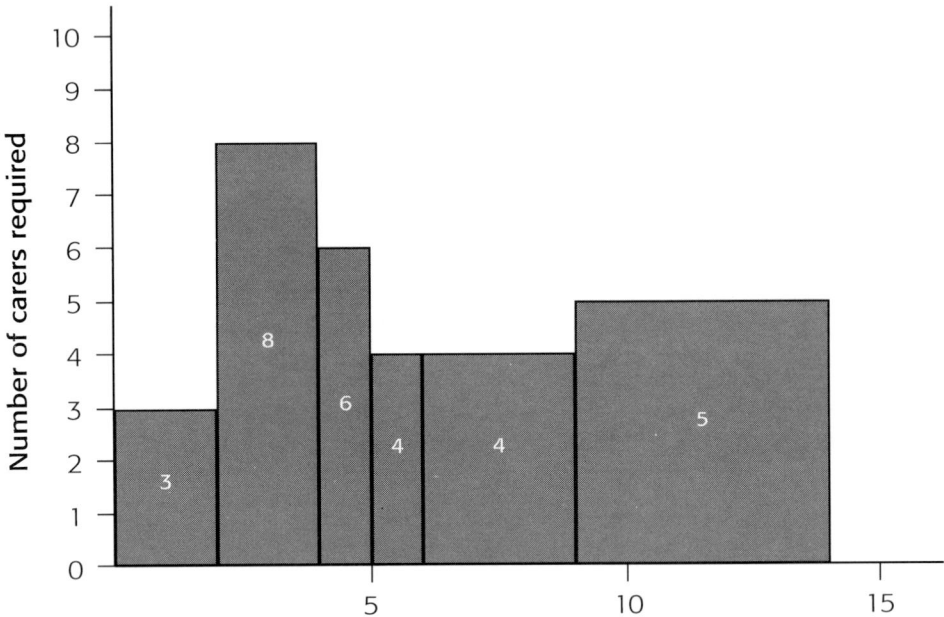

Figure 6.10

Suppose we only have six carers?

The completed histogram shows clearly that we do not have sufficient care staff between weeks 2 and 4. We need eight but only have six. This is where the float comes in.

If we study the bar chart we can see that by moving 'B' or 'D' i.e. doing one of them later, we can solve our resource problem. One solution is as follows – D has been moved so now has no float left, i.e., is 'critical' – but the resource problem is solved.

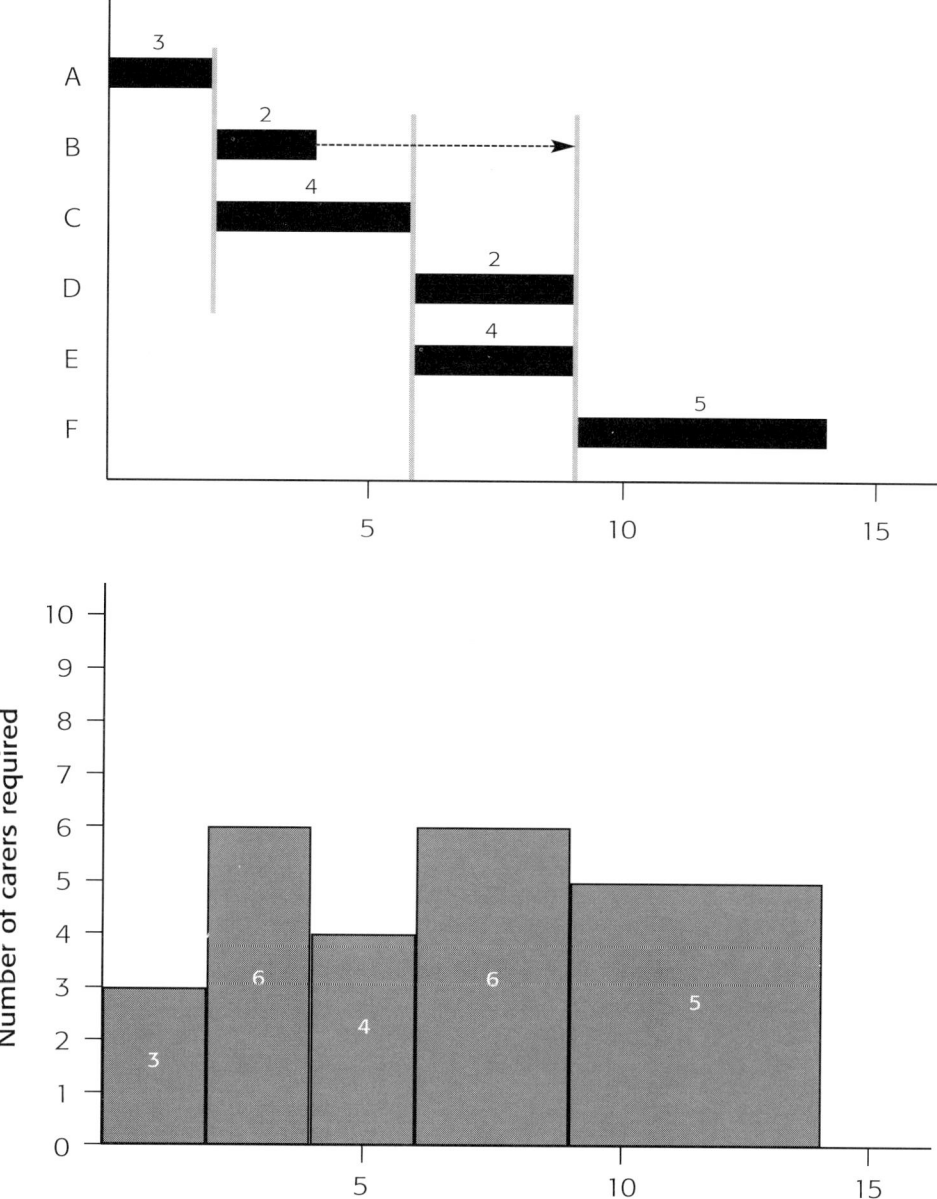

Figure 6.11

There are some other solutions you could use.

In deciding which one to move and how far to move it we need to take into account the cost of the work and how confident we feel about the work – a mini risk analysis in fact. If we plan to delay either activity 'B' or 'D' to their latest start dates this will solve our resource problem, but the activity will then be 'critical'. If we are confident about the activity, i.e. we feel that there is little risk, then this is acceptable especially if the activity is a high cost activity, because we will be spending our money as late as possible which is good management.

However, if the risk factor is high and the cost relatively low then perhaps we should just delay the activity a little, just enough to solve the resource problem, leaving some float in case the risk becomes a reality.

Work breakdown structures (WBS)

Work breakdown structures are simple diagrams or lists that show the elements or activities that go to make up a project. A WBS might look like Figure 6.12.

Notice that this schedule also lists materials and costs – hence we also have the budget.

Figure 6.12: Work breakdown structure for building a house

Activity No.	Activity	Duration (Days)	Resources		Cost (£)
			Labour (Man Days)	Materials	
01	Set Out	2	2 x Labourer	-	200
02	Foundations	6	12 x Labourers	2m³ Concrete	1800
03	Ground Floor Drains	3	6 x Labourers	20m Pipe	900
04	Ground Floor Slab	3	8 x Labourers	5m³ Concrete	1200
05	Walls	20	58 x Bricklayers	40,000 Bricks	10000
06	Roof	5	4 x Joiners 4 x Roofers	80m Felt 80m² Tiles	1000
07	Joinery	6	12 x Joiners	10 Doors 20 Windows	3000
08	Electrics	4	12 x Electricians	100m Cable 40 Fittings	1600
09	Plumbing	6	20 x Plumbers	100m Pipe 12 Radiators 1 Boiler	3000
10	Glazing	1	2 x Glazers	30m² Glass	200
12	Plastering	10	20 x Plasterers	100kg Plaster	2500
13	Decoration	8	16 x Decorators	100 litres Paint	2400
14	Clean and Tidy Site	4	4 x Labourer	-	400
-	Overheads	60	60 x Foreman	-	6000
				Total Cost =	34200

Or like that shown in Figure 6.13:

Figure 6.13: Task and resource list

ACTIVITY	Labourer	Electrician	Computer engineer	Carpenter/Plasterer	Painter/Decorator	Floor specialist	Project manager
1. Pre-work							
1.1 Design office layout							5
1.2 Obtain quotes							2
1.3 Gain authority to proceed							2
1.4 Confirm quotes							2
1.5 Order furniture							1
1.6 Order pictures and extras							1
1.7 Clear site	5						
2. Construction							
2.1 Fit false floor						15	
2.2 Build office partitions				10			
2.3 Painting and decorating					15		
3. Electrical							
3.1 Fit main cabling		8					
3.2 Electrical fittings		8					
4. Computers							
4.1 Fit IS cabling			10				
4.2 Install computer systems			5				
4.3 Install computer software			5				
5. Refurbishing							
5.1 Fit carpet						5	
5.2 Fit window blinds				5			
5.3 Position new desks	3						
5.4 Position new storage units	5						
5.5 Transfer office content	5						
5.6 Hang pictures etc.				2			
6. Sign off							
6.1 Check and fix						5	

Or even like that in Figure 6.14:

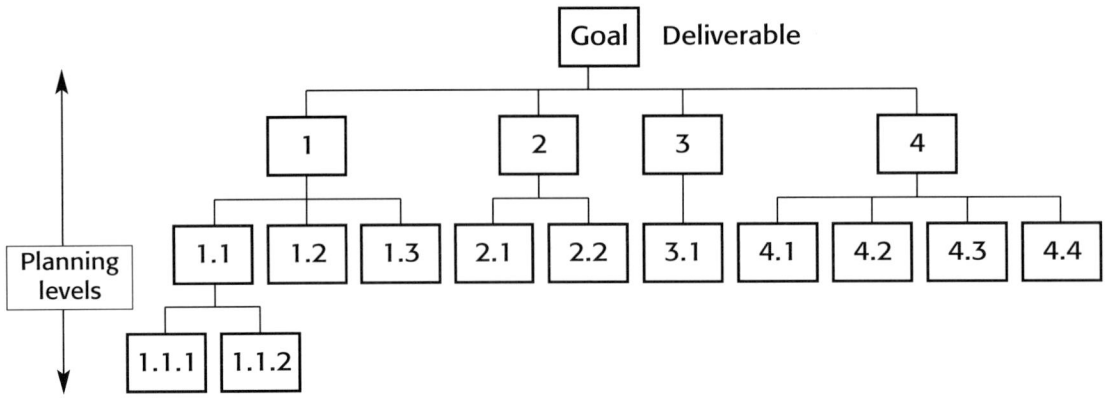

Figure 6.14

Work-to lists or schedules

As the name implies, these are lists for people to work to. They list the tasks to be done, when they can start and when they must be completed. They come in many guises but a simple one would look like this:

Activity	Discipline	Person	Start date	Finish date	Notes
Evaluate service	transport	Bloggs	week 27	week 28	Delayed queries to resolve
Order service	transport	Brown	week 31	week 32	Waiting for data from finance

The above is a basic work-to list. Clearly it is possible to make them more elaborate. The choice is yours. The guiding principle is to let the project nature and complexity be your guide and keep all documentation as simple as possible.

Milestone charts

A milestone chart is a chart on which only milestones are shown. Milestones mark key points in a project – usually designated by this symbol *. In the case of a major project such as introducing a new product/service, milestones might be:

- board approval
- product design complete
- product text in specified area complete
- handbooks and operating instructions in use in all sections
- training course designed
- publicity material produced

For a building project the chart might look like this:

Figure 6.15: Milestone chart

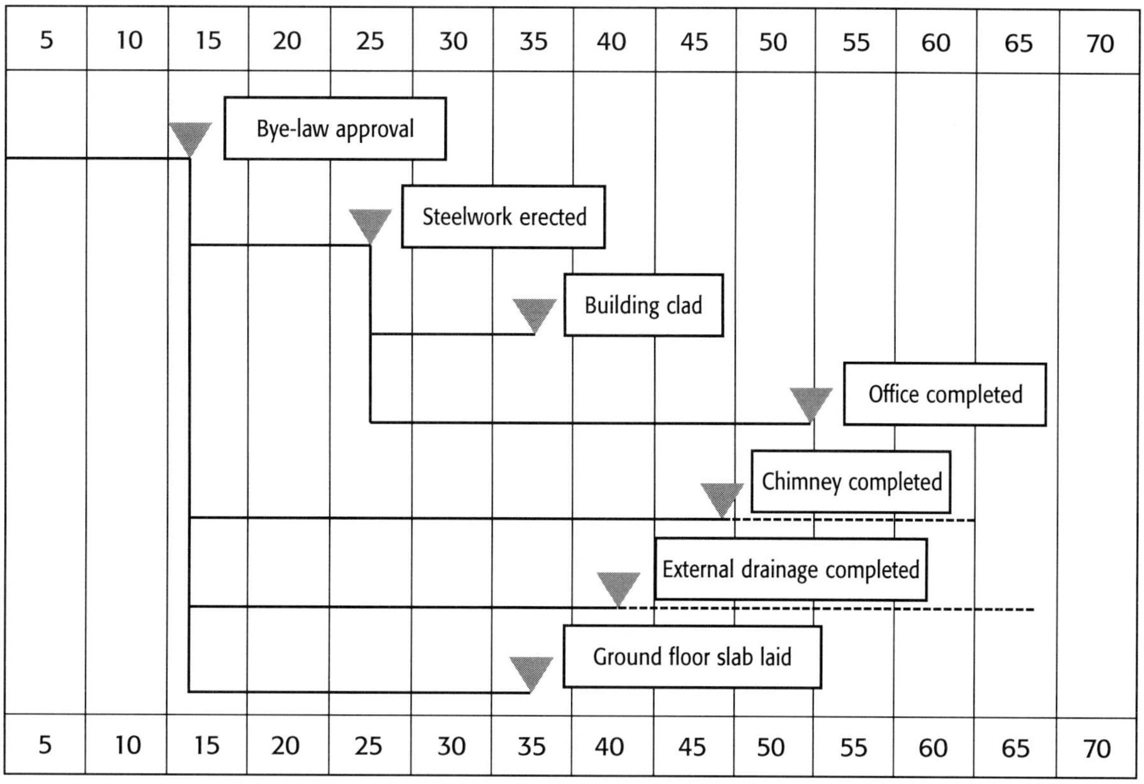

5	10	15	20	25	30	35	40	45	50	55	60	65	70

Bye-law approval

Steelwork erected

Building clad

Office completed

Chimney completed

External drainage completed

Ground floor slab laid

5	10	15	20	25	30	35	40	45	50	55	60	65	70

Milestone management

Having established the milestones, it is possible to use them as a means of overall control of the project. For milestone management to be successful the milestones should be significant events where there is no doubt as to whether the event has occurred. Each of the above milestones occurs when an activity or job is completed and there should be a tangible way of checking to see that these have been accomplished.

Avoid using milestones that do not have a tangible result, e.g. 'Safety procedures dispatched to all area offices.' This would be better if replaced by a milestone such as 'Safety procedures received and implemented by all area offices.' Remember that too many milestones will only devalue their importance. For a major project about 10 milestones should be all that are needed.

If you have too many milestones in a project, it usually means that the project needs more planning.

When to use which planning tool

The project board is responsible for making the decisions that will lead to the design of the plans, but in practice it is the project manager's role to choose the planning tools and methods for project board approval.

When designing a plan, the project manager needs to bear in mind the scale of the project and answer the following questions:

- What planning, estimating, monitoring and risk assessment methods will be used?
- What tools (such as IT software) should be used to help with planning, estimating, monitoring and risk assessment?
- What level of detail about the services, their creation, quality checks and plan monitoring is required for day-to-day control?
- What level of detail does the project board need:
  - before commitment to a plan?
  - to monitor progress against the plan?
- How will any quality checks be shown on the plans, in particular sign-off?
- How will the training and mentoring needs of the team be addressed?

Armed with the above information the project manager is in a position to decide which planning tools to use. The plans necessary for managing the project will need to reflect the circumstances and scale of each project.

For a small project, say 8 to 20 activities, you may only need to list the activities such as a work-to list, on a WBS or a milestone chart. For a slightly more complex project, where the individual tasks are of longer duration you may find that a bar chart will be sufficient. However, as you get to projects involving around 30 or more activities you will need to use networks to help you plan and control the project.

For high priority projects it is likely that a combination of all the types of plan mentioned will be required to manage the project effectively. At this point you should consider using an IT programme to aid you.

Computers

Computers are least useful on small projects and in the planning stages of projects as they cannot show the overall picture even when projected onto a large screen. They come into their own as the projects increase in size or complexity and when regular up-dates and reports are required. As with all things it is a case of 'horses for courses'.

There are many computer programs available. If you are doing regular project up-dates or if you are running large or multiple interconnected projects you should invest the time to learn to use one of the many project management packages that are on the market.

However, the over-riding principle involved here is that the programs cannot manage the project for you! Unless you are well versed and properly trained to use an IT package you will often find that it is more trouble than it is worth. This is not an anti-IT stance, just a hard learned piece of advice.

All the techniques discussed can be done manually and most of them need to be done with the whole group present.

Summary

 There is a saying – 'To fail to plan is to plan to fail'.
There is another saying – 'Isn't it great when a plan comes together.'

Planning is important because it increases understanding and enables control. However, it is vital to exercise control, that is take corrective action, when it is indicated. Before moving on to deal with financial planning and budgeting, you may wish to work through the following exercise.

A worked example

Scenario

You decide to embark on a self-build house project. Many things will need to be done. Land will need to be found and purchased. Many legal aspects will need to be dealt with, finance will need to be arranged and there will be a myriad of things to do. Here we will deal only with on aspect of the project – the actual build.

You and your partner sit down and work out the steps in the process. Using pieces of paper – or post-its. You make out a post-it for each operation. At this stage you try to look at the big picture and not go into too much detail. Then you lay out the post-its in logical order, i.e. the sequence that you think the project must take, bearing in mind the dependencies. Your network at this stage might look like Figure 6.16.

First the plot must be marked out. Then the foundations and the drains can be worked on simultaneously. Once these are done the concrete for the ground floor slab can be poured and when this is dry the walls can be built. Once the walls are up, the roof, the electrics, joinery and plumbing can all be worked on simultaneously. When the joinery is done, the glazing can go in. Once the glazing is done and the roof is complete, the building can be said to be weather-tight – a milestone. When the building is weather-tight, plastering can be done – but only if the electrics and plumbing are complete. When the plaster is dry, we can decorate. Then we clean up the site and we have finished.

Having drawn the network, we can examine it to satisfy ourselves that it is correct. Any changes to the logic can be made until we are sure that the diagram is a true picture of the way the project goes together.

Be clear that, later in the project, you will almost certainly change the network. Also, later in the project, you may discover that some of the dependencies were wrong or had been misunderstood. This is normal – but it does not invalidate the work you have done. By drawing the network and thinking through the logic you will have gained a great understanding of your project that will prove invaluable as the project later unfolds.

Having sorted out the logic we can now address timings.

First number each box in the top left hand corner, then ask the appropriate person to give you an estimate of the time for each of the activities. Write these on the bottom left hand corner of the 'notes'. Having done this your project plan will look like Figure 6.17.

Notice that 'building weather-tight' and 'house complete' are milestones – important points in the building process – and are shown with zero duration time.

Using these figures we can calculate the 'earliest finish time' (EFT) for each activity which we record in the top right hand corner. So foundations can be completed in eight weeks (2+6), whereas drains can be completed by week 5 (2 + 3). The ground floor slab takes three weeks but cannot be worked on until drains and foundations are in place. Foundations we know are not complete until week 8 so the earliest we can finish the ground floor slab is week 11.

Moving on through the diagram in this way shows that completion time for the project is 60 weeks. Our diagram now looks like Figure 6.18.

Figure 6.16: Basic network showing dependencies

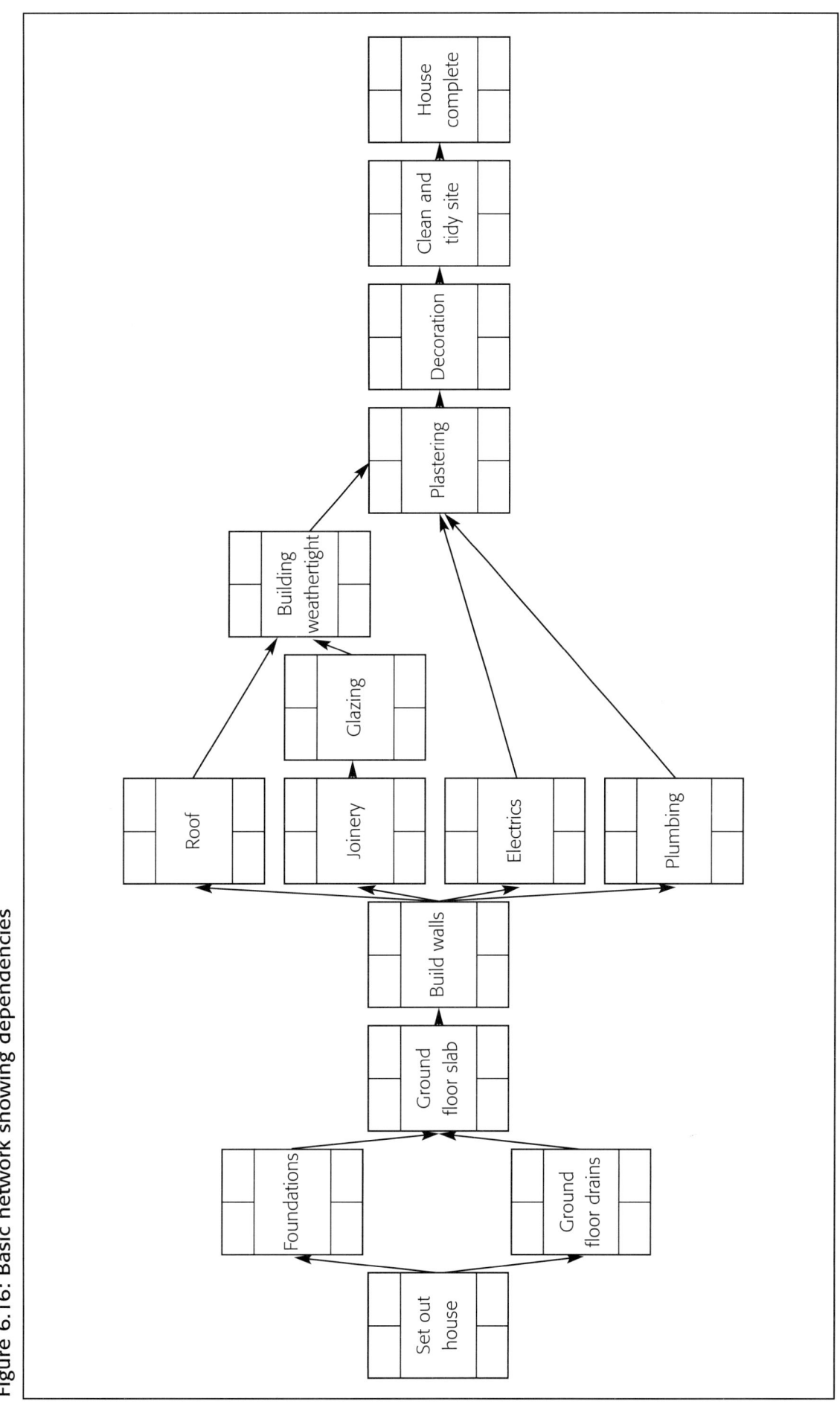

Figure 6.17: Basic network with numbered boxes and duration times added

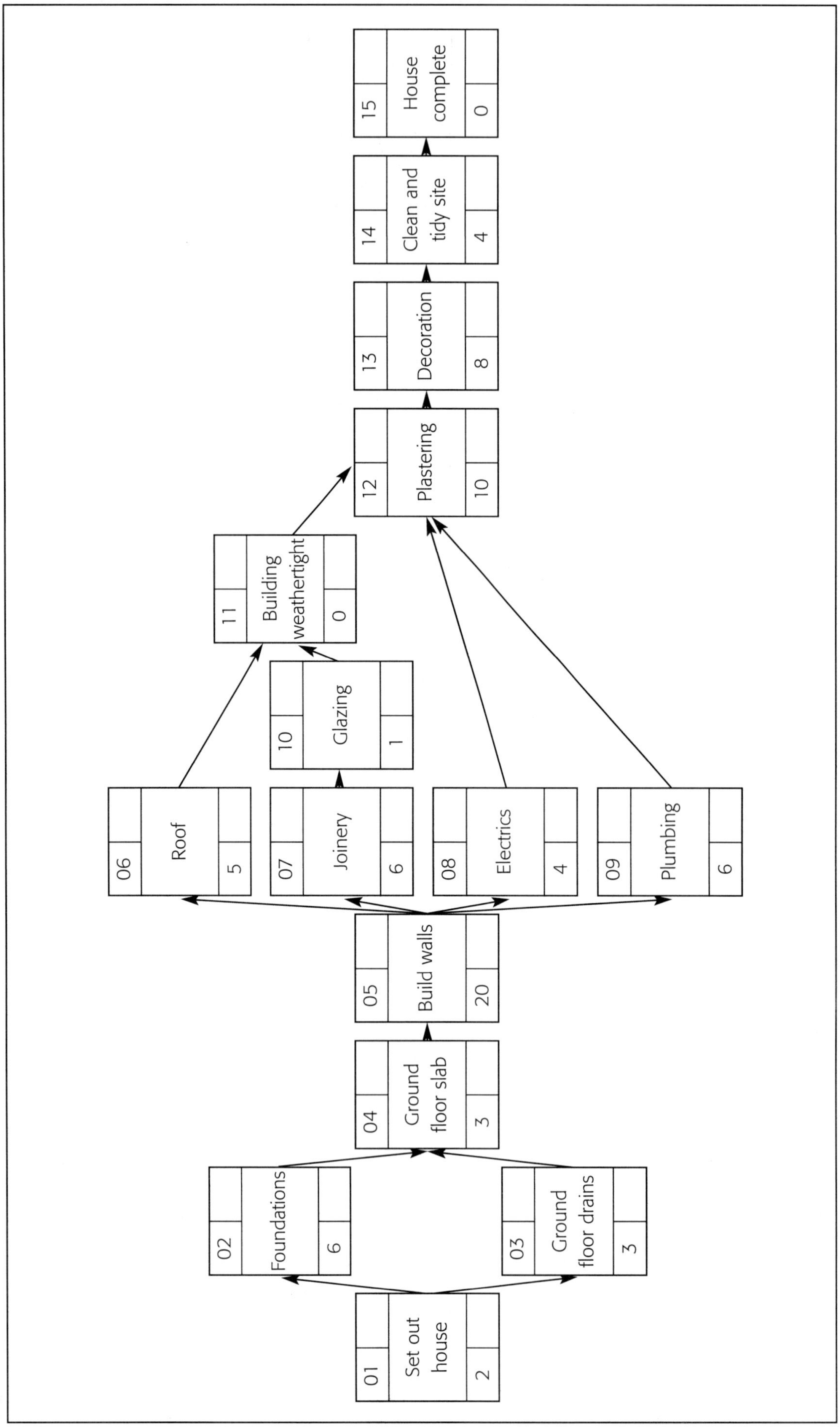

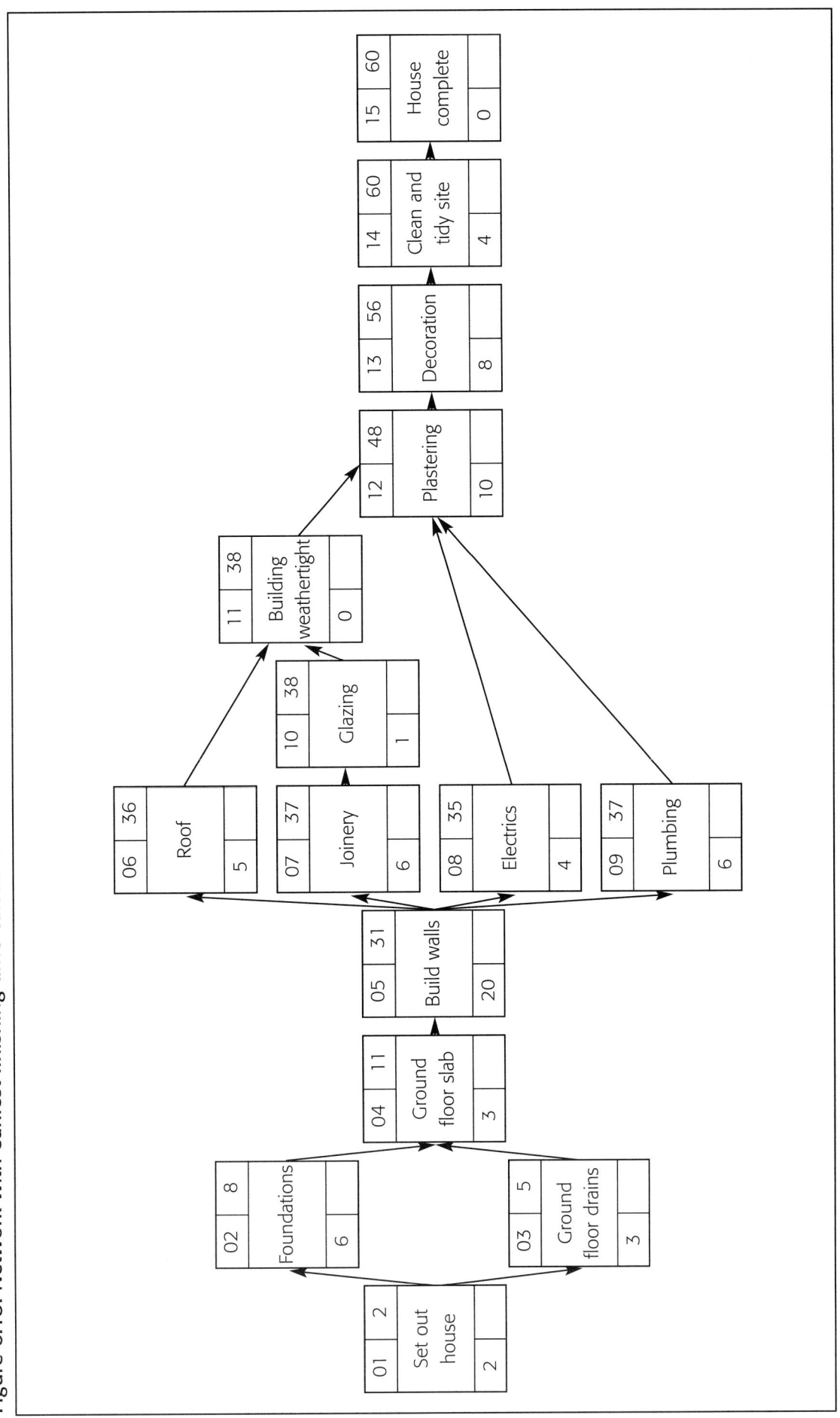

Figure 6.18: Network with earliest finishing time calculated

Working back from house complete, we can now fill in the latest completion times for each activity. These are entered in the bottom right hand square. Notice that the roof can be completed by week 36 (EFT) but need not be finished until week 38 (LFT) because the glazing will not be complete until then. Similarly, 'ground floor drains' need not be completed until week 8 because the laying of the ground floor slab cannot commence until the foundations are done (week 8).

The difference between the EFT for an activity and the LFT is called 'float'. Activities that have no float are called critical activities. The critical activities control the time that a project will take, hence the term critical path. The completed network should look like Figure 6.19.

All networks have a critical path. Some networks have more than one critical path. During the life of a project the critical path may change. This is normal. The key thing is to know where the critical path is at any time so that, as project manager, emphasis can be given to the appropriate activities.

We now have our network and in all probability the WBS has been created at the same time. If it hasn't we can at least begin to construct it putting in the information that we have at present. Eventually the completed WBS will look like Figure 6.20.

In the example shown we have also added a column in which we have the costings – so our budget is also done! Later we can use a modified version of this document as a progress and reporting document.

Having thought out the dependencies – i.e. the logic for building the house – and drawn the network, we can show this in the form of a bar chart if we wish, see Figure 6.21.

Each activity is drawn to scale horizontally and any float is shown by a dotted line, or grey area. If we look at 'ground floor drains' we can see that it can start on week 2 and finish on week 5 (EFT). However the grey area tells us that if we wish we can reschedule this activity so long as it is finished by week 8. The critical activities are clearly shown – they have no grey areas or float and 'building weather-tight' and 'house complete' milestones are represented by triangles.

We can further improve the bar chart by adding the vertical dependency lines – see Figure 6.22. These show the relationships between activities more clearly.

A further refinement of the bar chart is a resource schedule – see Figure 6.23.

Here are added a row for each of the various skill groups and on the bar chart the number of people required for each job has been added. So we can see that between the end of week 2 and the end of week 4 we require one foreman and four labourers. In week 31 there will be one bricklayer required, plus the foreman. In week 32 we need two roofers, two joiners, two electricians and a plumber, plus of course the foreman.

The network we have been working on is quite small and is simple. Larger networks are – just larger. They are still as simple. If you can draw and understand a small network you are capable of drawing and understanding large networks. Many people say that if a project has less than 30 activities it is not worth drawing a network. However, it takes so little time to draw a small network that it is foolish not to draw one.

The benefits of understanding the **logic** of a project **before** doing the planning cannot be overstated.

Figure 6.19: Finished network, with critical path highlighted

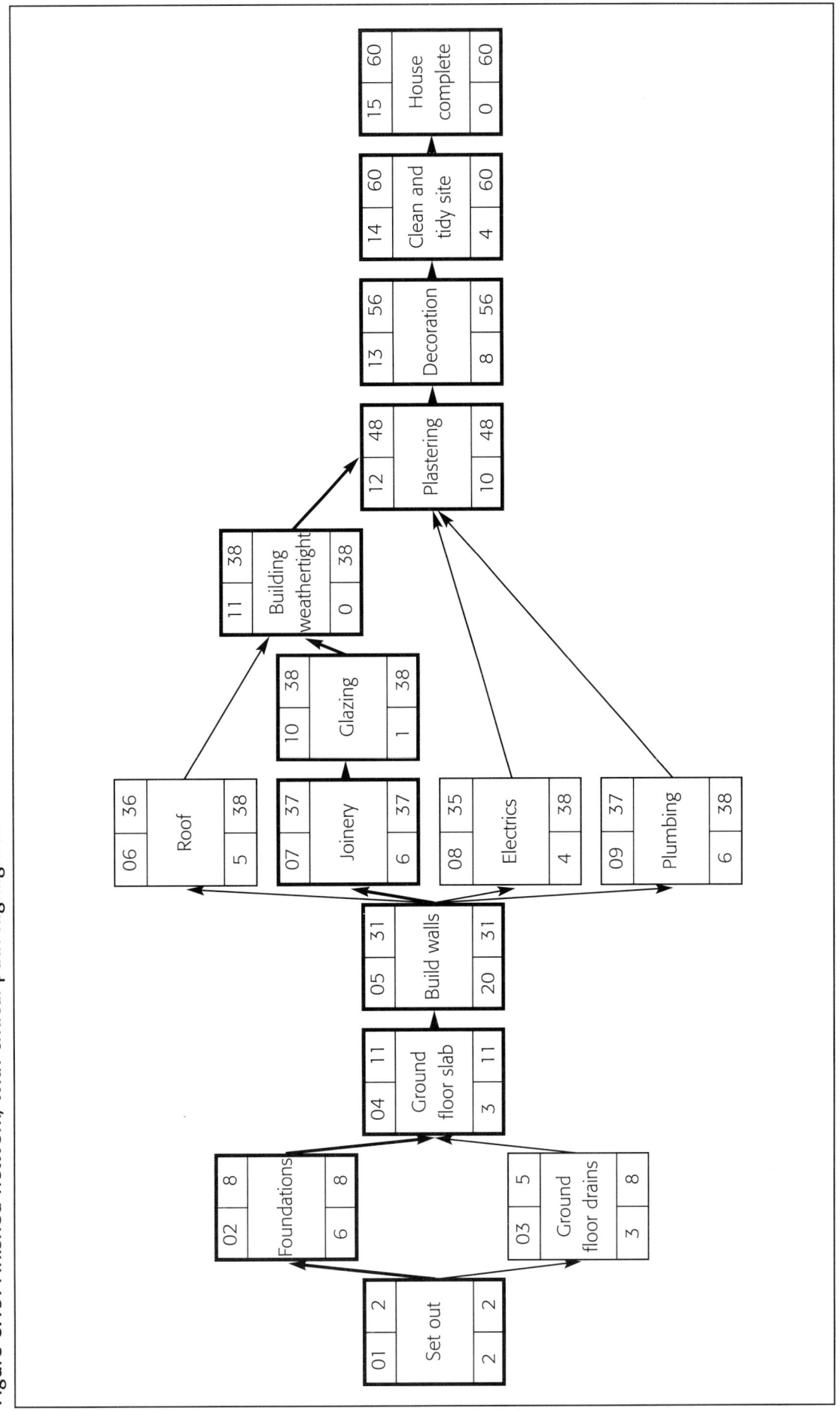

Figure 6.20

Activity No.	Activity	Duration (Days)	Labour (Man Days)	Materials	Cost (£)
				Resources	
01	Set Out	2	2 x Labourer	-	200
02	Foundations	6	12 x Labourers	2m³ Concrete	1800
03	Ground Floor Drains	3	6 x Labourers	20m Pipe	900
04	Ground Floor Slab	3	8 x Labourers	5m³ Concrete	1200
05	Walls	20	58 x Bricklayers	40,000 Bricks	10000
06	Roof	5	4 x Joiners 4 x Roofers	80m Felt 80m² Tiles	1000
07	Joinery	6	12 x Joiners	10 Doors 20 Windows	3000
08	Electrics	4	12 x Electricians	100m Cable 40 Fittings	1600
09	Plumbing	6	20 x Plumbers	100m Pipe 12 Radiators 1 Boiler	3000
10	Glazing	1	2 x Glazers	30m² Glass	200
12	Plastering	10	20 x Plasterers	100kg Plaster	2500
13	Decoration	8	16 x Decorators	100 litres Paint	2400
14	Clean and Tidy Site	4	4 x Labourer	-	400
-	Overheads	60	60 x Foreman	-	6000
				Total Cost =	34200

Figure 6.21: Bar chart for building a house

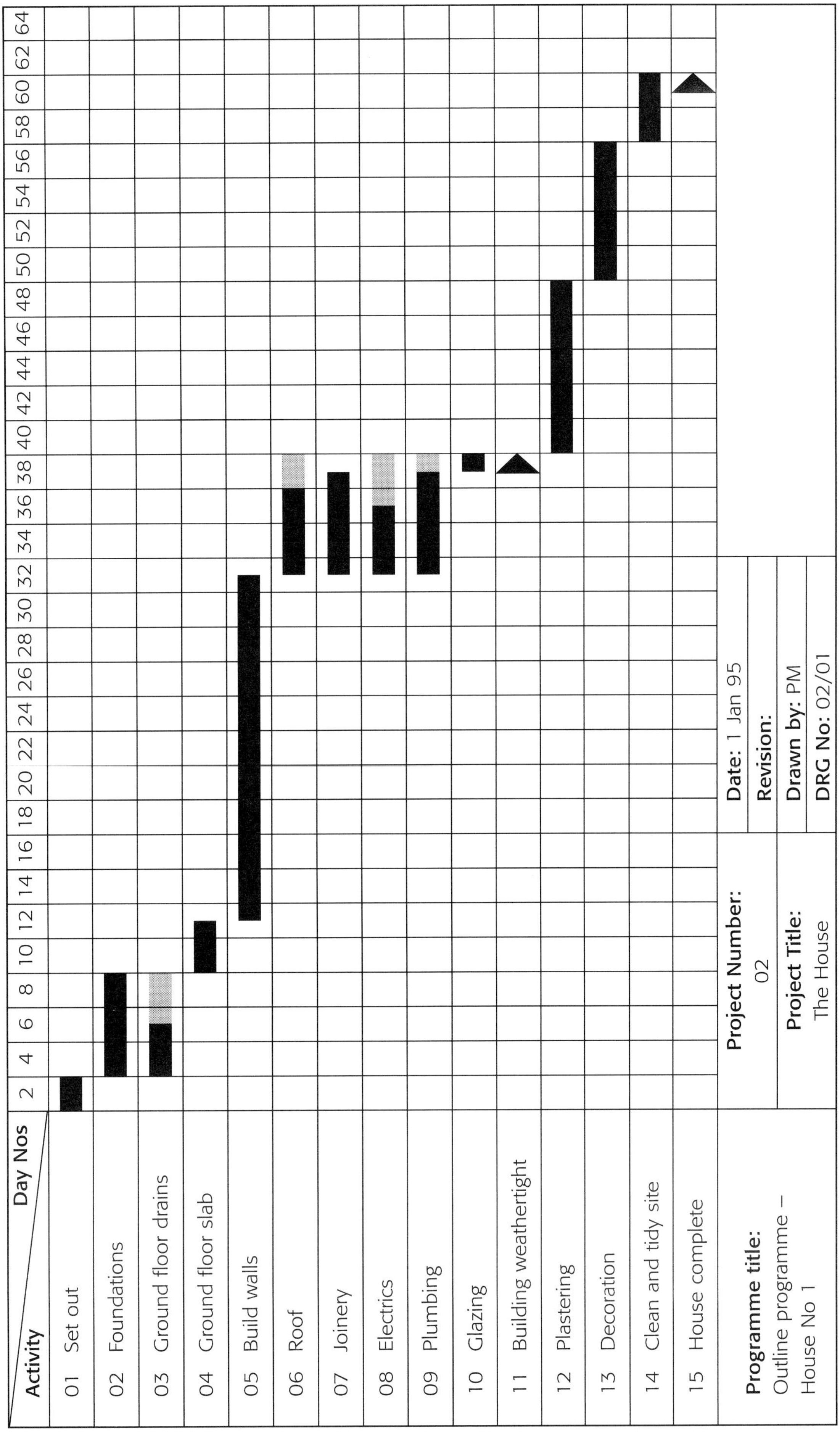

Activity	Day Nos
01 Set out	
02 Foundations	
03 Ground floor drains	
04 Ground floor slab	
05 Build walls	
06 Roof	
07 Joinery	
08 Electrics	
09 Plumbing	
10 Glazing	
11 Building weathertight	
12 Plastering	
13 Decoration	
14 Clean and tidy site	
15 House complete	

Programme title: Outline programme – House No 1	Project Number: 02	Date: 1 Jan 95
	Project Title: The House	Revision:
		Drawn by: PM
		DRG No: 02/01

Figure 6.22: Bar chart for building a house

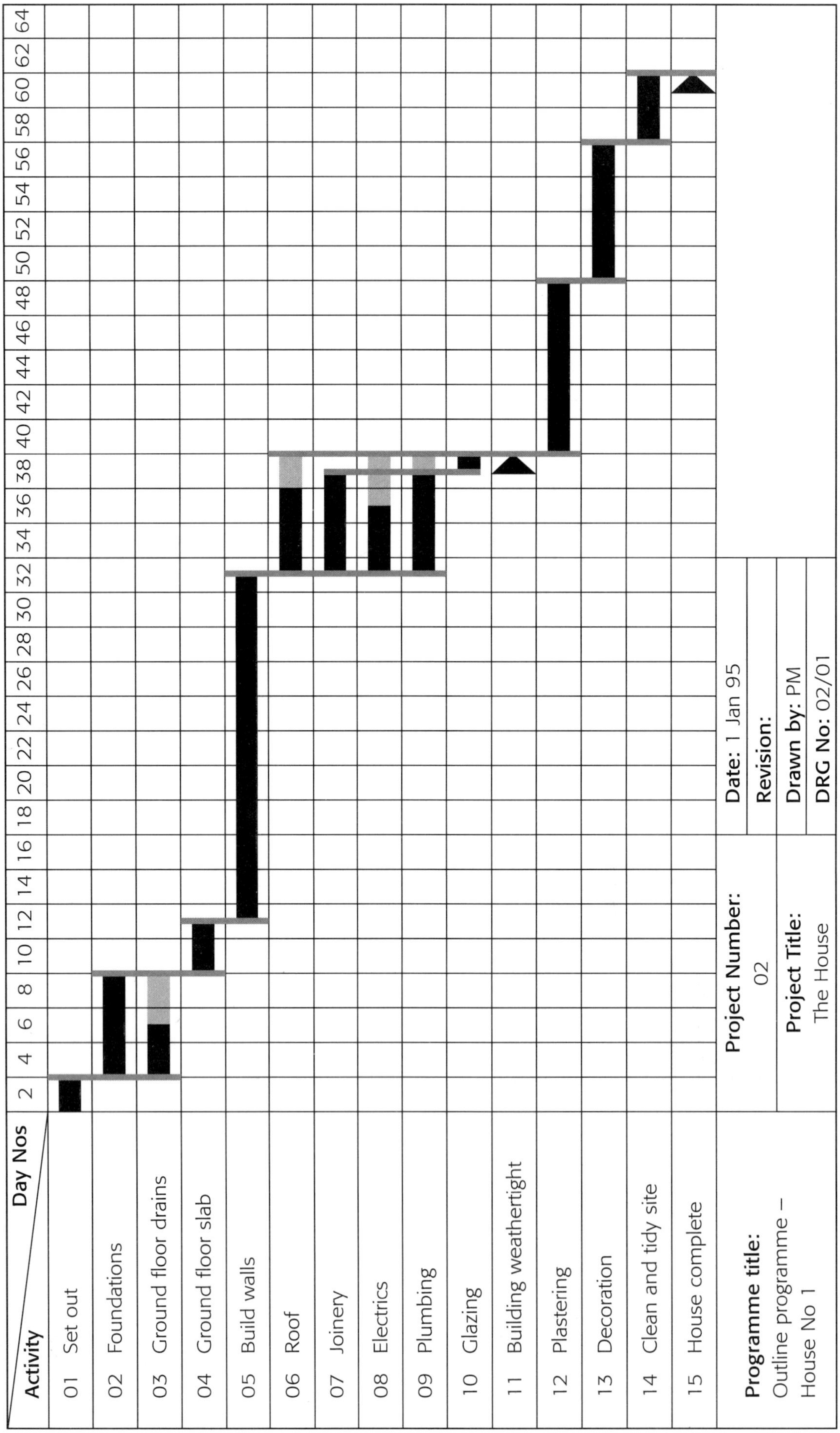

Day Nos	2	4	6	8	10	12	14	16	18	20	22	24	26	28	30	32	34	36	38	40	42	44	46	48	50	52	54	56	58	60	62	64

Activity

01 Set out
02 Foundations
03 Ground floor drains
04 Ground floor slab
05 Build walls
06 Roof
07 Joinery
08 Electrics
09 Plumbing
10 Glazing
11 Building weathertight
12 Plastering
13 Decoration
14 Clean and tidy site
15 House complete

Project Number:	Date: 1 Jan 95
02	Revision:
Project Title:	Drawn by: PM
The House	DRG No: 02/01

Programme title:
Outline programme –
House No 1

72

Figure 6.23: Resourced bar chart

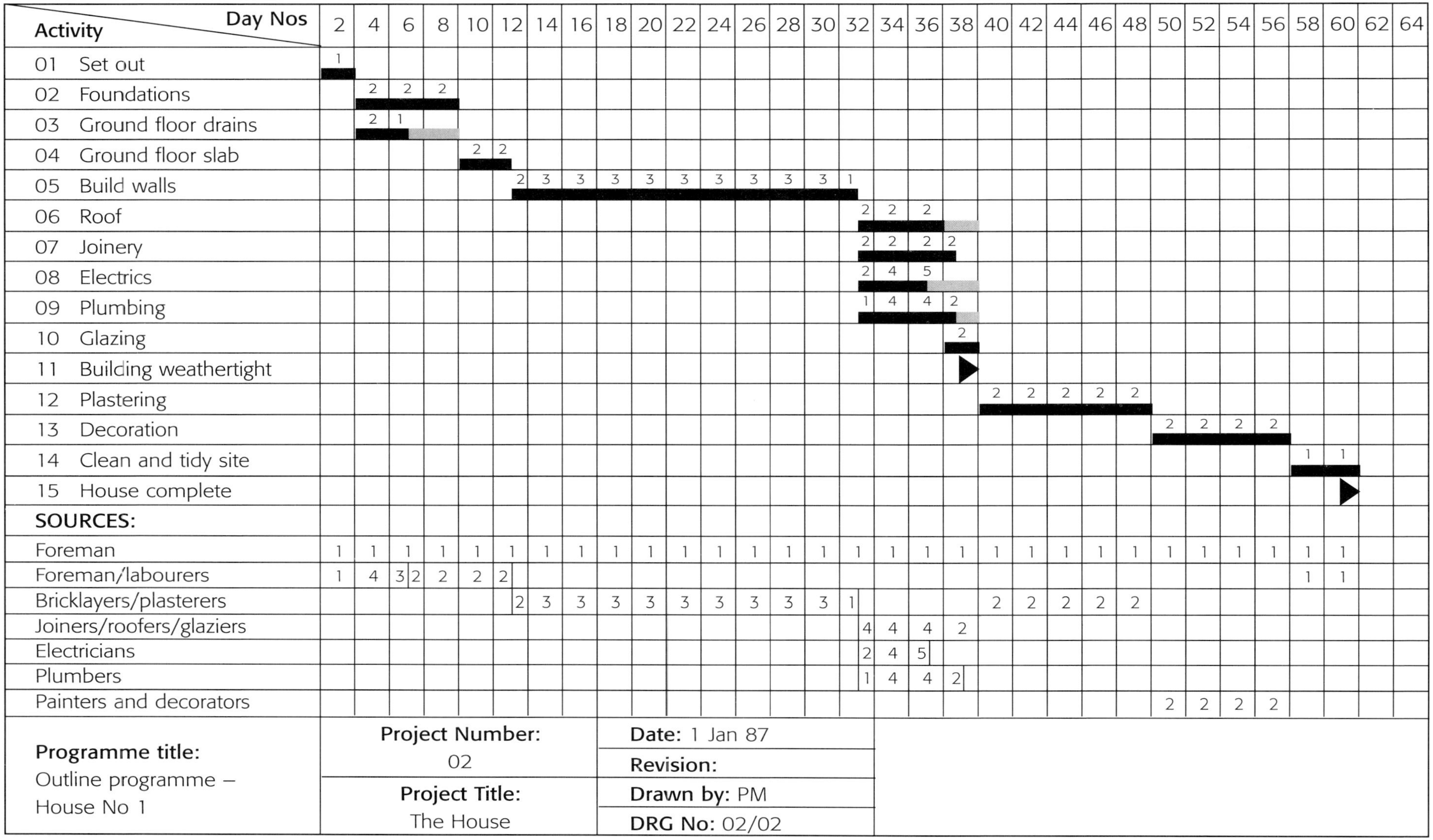

Activity	Day Nos	2	4	6	8	10	12	14	16	18	20	22	24	26	28	30	32	34	36	38	40	42	44	46	48	50	52	54	56	58	60	62	64

01 Set out
02 Foundations
03 Ground floor drains
04 Ground floor slab
05 Build walls
06 Roof
07 Joinery
08 Electrics
09 Plumbing
10 Glazing
11 Building weathertight
12 Plastering
13 Decoration
14 Clean and tidy site
15 House complete

SOURCES:
Foreman
Foreman/labourers
Bricklayers/plasterers
Joiners/roofers/glaziers
Electricians
Plumbers
Painters and decorators

Programme title: Outline programme – House No 1

Project Number: 02
Project Title: The House
Date: 1 Jan 87
Revision:
Drawn by: PM
DRG No: 02/02

73

Exercise and suggested answer

A drop-in centre

A friend of yours has been asked to open a drop-in centre and has asked you to help plan the project. She thinks that it will take her three weeks to prepare and submit a proposal to the voluntary organisation and a further week for them to decide whether or not to grant the funding.

Locating the right premises will take about five weeks plus a further three weeks to finalise negotiations on the lease. Once the money is approved the lease can be signed immediately and the building taken over within four weeks. After moving in, another three weeks will be needed to decorate and put up new signs.

Your friend is going to be the manager and two or three workers will need to be recruited. Advertising for staff will take three weeks and interviewing and vetting will take a further two weeks. The staff will be appointed as soon as the lease is signed. Once appointed, however, the new staff will have to work two weeks notice with their present employer.

New furniture and equipment will be required and quotations are expected to take two weeks. These items will not be purchased until the lease is signed. Delivery time for the furniture and equipment is four weeks.

Final fitting and cleaning of the premises will take one week. Before the opening, advertisements will be placed in the local press for a week. The new sign must be in place before the advertisements appear. Somewhere in the project plan allow two weeks in case something should go wrong.

Your task is to prepare a network diagram for this project. How many weeks will it take from the start of this project to the grand opening? Which activities are critical? Prepare a bar chart for the project, and briefly explain what you think are the greatest risks to the project.

Suggested answers are shown in Figures 6.24 and 6.25. Your answer may be different from the suggested answer. Remember, your answer is the right answer because that is the way you are managing the project. However, here are some pointers that might be useful.

Some people think that the proposal and the premises must be sorted before funding is agreed. Others take the view that a general proposal outlining the major costs and funding can be submitted and approved in principle before the detail is sorted out as in arranging a mortgage, where the loan is approved, based on income, before a house has been located. Some people take the view that premises cannot be located or leases negotiated until the charity has made a decision, again that view is not shared in the suggested answer.

Appointing staff – just a phone call, followed by a letter, is shown by a milestone – and is not the same as staff joining the payroll. If you wanted to you could have staff on the payroll by week 10, but in all possibility you will agree a start date of week 17, or week 16 if some training was necessary.

The two weeks' contingency has been added – to prepare proposal, 1 week, and final fitting, 1 week. Notice that as 'prepare proposal' is not on the critical path, the project duration is only extended by one week.

If 'final fitting' was left as a 1 week activity in the above network then the completion date would be week 16 and there would be two critical paths, one through final fitting and one through press advertisement. It is not unusual to have more than one critical path.

Note that on the bar chart some activities do not appear to have their float shown – prepare proposal for example. This is deliberate because the finance is dependent on 'prepare proposal' and the two activities share the same float. 'Advertise for staff' and 'Interview staff' also share the same float.

Figure 6.24: Project network – drop-in centre

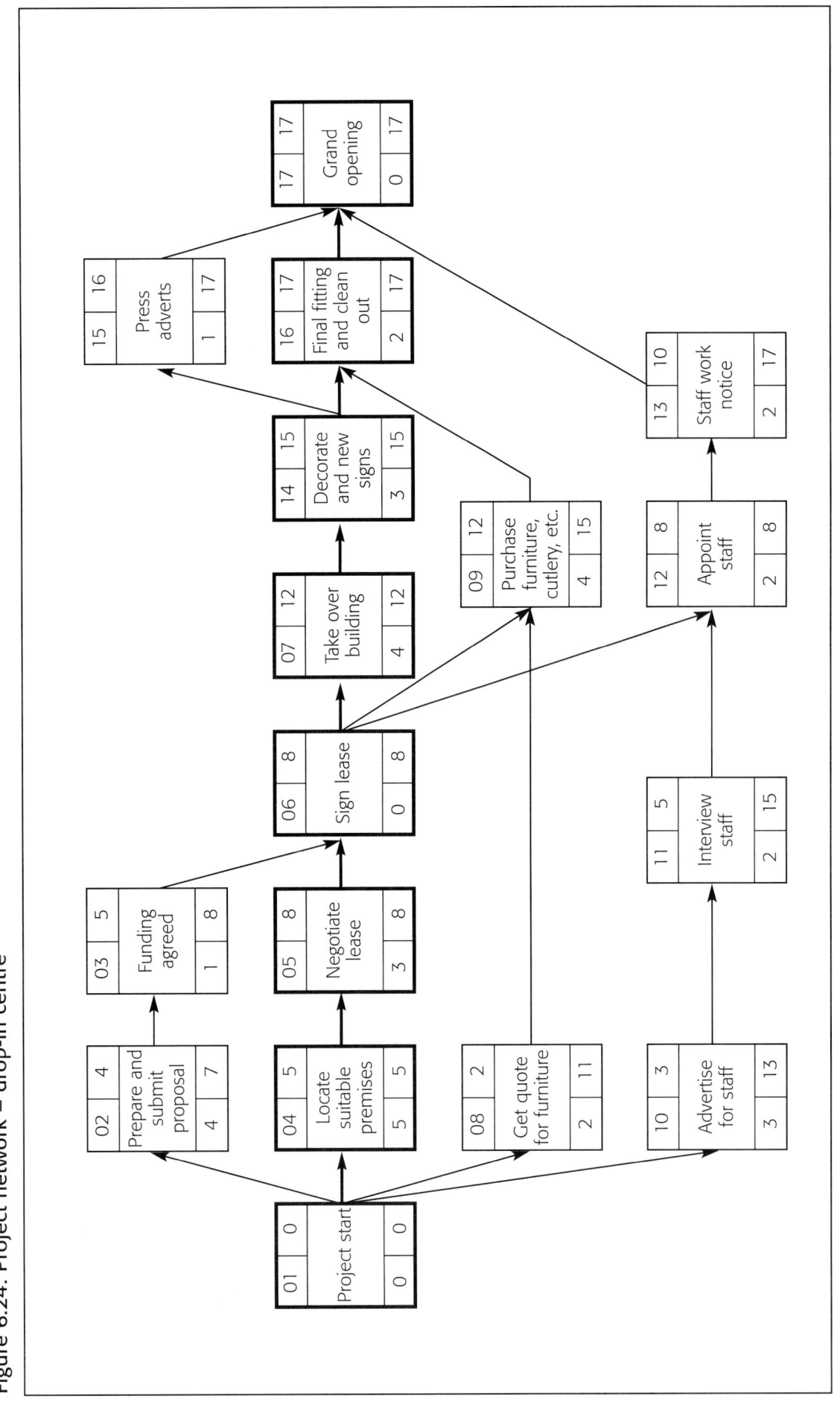

Figure 6.25: Drop-in centre – bar chart

Activity	Week No	1	2	3	4	5	6	7	8	9	10	11	12	13	14	15	16	17	18	19	20
01	Project start																				
02	Prepare and submit proposal																				
03	Funding agreed																				
04	Locate premises																				
05	Negotiate lease																				
06	Sign lease																				
07	Take over building																				
08	Get quotes furniture																				
09	Purchase furniture, etc.																				
10	Advertise for staff																				
11	Interview staff																				
12	Appoint staff																				
13	Staff work notice																				
14	Decorate and new sign																				
15	Press adverts																				
16	Final fit and clean out																				
17	Grand opening																				

Programme title:	Project Number:	Date:	Revision:
Drop-in centre	Project Title:	Drawn by:	DRG No:

Chapter 7
The Planning Stage: The Budget

The importance of the project budget

Having a well-prepared budget makes it easy to monitor and control a project. In commercial projects the budget is perhaps the most important and most used planning and control tool. The budget is key because it is often the basis on which the decision on whether or not to proceed with the project is made. Clearly, if funds are limited a project may be abandoned at an early stage. That is unless there are other factors in the equation, such as the need to be seen to be operating in a certain marketplace, or the fact that the project must go ahead regardless of cost, for example, combating the foot and mouth epidemic in the UK. Hence it is vital that the budget preparation is properly carried out. A poorly put together budget could cause a potentially profitable project to be turned down, or it could lure an organisation into embarking on a project that would eventually lead to losses being made.

The lack of a budget mentality

What if there is no budget mentality in your place of work? Many people say that they have no access to information about costs and that budgets are not required for their projects, or if they are, someone else prepares them and they are not available to the project manager.

 If there is a project budget then the project manager should be heavily involved in its preparation. It is part of the project definition process.

Even where a project budget is not a requirement, and many organisations tackle projects using existing staff and choose not to allocate times to individual projects, there is still a case for the project manager to produce a budget. If you have no access to cost information then show costs as 'hours of work' for individuals and include management time. It is good practice to get into the habit of budgeting even if you are not required to do so.

Many people are happy to proceed without a budget. If you have no budget you cannot fail to meet the budget. However, it really is important to prepare one.

 Example

An outside consultant was appointed on a one day a week basis, for approximately a year, to implement a user participation scheme within an organisation. No budget was produced but contained within the consultant's monthly report was a statement of money spent, including her own time. Despite numerous requests for details of finances available none was forthcoming. However, during month nine the consultant was called to see the head of department who informed her that all the allocated money for the project had been used up which meant that unfortunately her services would no longer be required.

Common budgeting problems

Many people are put off budgeting or choose to avoid the budgeting issue because of the difficulties involved in preparing a sound budget. In some cases it is because the first attempt at budgeting went so wrong that they have lost confidence in their ability to budget. The more you do it the better you will become and you will be surprised at how quickly you improve. Having said that, there are some well-known difficulties that need confronting, the main ones being:

- Unreliable estimates.
- Managers secretly adding in contingency.
- Senior managers cutting the budget.
- Overlooking tasks.
- Not having enough time to prepare the budget.

How can we deal with these difficulties?

Unreliable estimates are given from time to time. Sometimes it is not the estimator's fault but the fault of the person specifying the work to be done. A poor specification leads to a poor estimate. When specifying work to be done remember the basics of project definition and key success criteria and you will reduce the chance of poor specification.

Managers sometimes add in contingency to a budget on the 'I didn't get where I am today without knowing a bit about project budgeting' basis. They are entitled to do this of course, but two things are important here. One is that they should be open about what they are doing and discuss it with the project manager. The other is that the extra money is targeted so that it is clear what the contingency is for. The way to show this is to record it in the contingency log and add it to the contingency part of the budget.

Managers can also trim a budget. They can do so because they think, in their experience, a budget has been produced that is too high. Again, this is fine so long as the logic behind the trimming is discussed with the project manager and this has been recorded. Clearly, if the trimming is too fierce, the project manager must decide his or her position! Sometimes a manager will trim a budget just to task the project manager. They will take 10-15% out of the budget and challenge the project manager to make savings. It is called an incentive by these managers. It rather depends on your management style and views about motivation as to whether or not you agree with this approach.

Tasks can be overlooked. In fact it is more correct to say that tasks **will** be overlooked. But less will be overlooked if you budget than if you do not budget. When tasks are overlooked we all feel stupid, but again that is no justification for not budgeting. The more you do it the fewer tasks will be overlooked. Split your team into two groups when you prepare your budget. Let each group work separately at first, then bring them together and compare the budgets each group has produced. This is a good safeguard against missing items but it is not foolproof. Remember, the budget must be 'signed off' so if things have been missed, they have been missed by all the parties to the signing off.

Not having enough time to do a budget is rather like saying that there is not enough time to do the project. Budgeting is part of the planning process. Without planning the project is not being project managed. The project manager should insist that adequate time and resources are allocated so that a proper budget can be prepared.

Types of budget

There are two main methods for preparing a budget. These are:

- top-down budgeting
- bottom-up budgeting

Top-down budgeting

A top-down budget is one where the final cost is known in advance and is usually an amount of money set on a 'must not exceed' basis. An example might be a conference, a launch party, a design programme, and where the figure is set at the beginning.

In top-down budgeting, the key to producing the final budget is the understanding of the work breakdown structure (WBS). Often the work breakdown structure is not in place but is developed simultaneously along with the budget as in the following example.

You are asked to put on a conference. Your budget is £20,000. At this point your WBS will look as simple as 'Conference complete, £20,000'. You must now consider the elements that need to be in place to ensure a successful conference.

You decide that there are four key areas – the venue, the speakers, the delegates and the marketing. You think that you can get four speakers for £2,000 plus their accommodation and travel costs making the total £3,200. There is now £16,800 to split amongst the rest. If we allow £6k for the venue and a further £6k for delegates' expenses we have £4,800 left for marketing. Our WBS now looks like this:

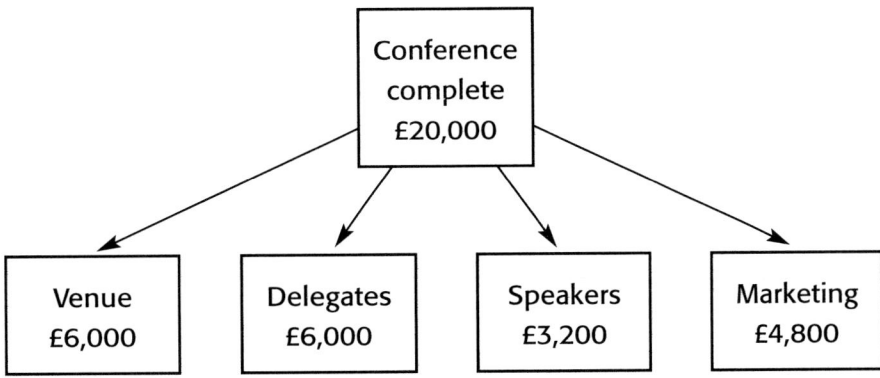

Figure 7.1

79

We can now proceed to take each item and further break down the costs, for example we can split the delegates' cost into travelling costs, accommodation costs and subsistence, if we wish. It depends on the level of detail that is required.

Bottom-up budgeting

A bottom-up budget, as you would imagine, is the reverse of a top-down budget. Here we build up the budget from the bottom, item by item, detail by detail, line by line.

If we are planning an activities holiday for young offenders, then, using top-down budgeting, we might say there is a total fund of £10,000 and we then proceed as in the example above. On the other hand we could approach the problem from the bottom up, in which case we would produce a detailed specification for the holiday, including type of accommodation such as camping or self-catering, venue – France or Great Yarmouth, number of days, time of year and so on. Then we build up the costs:

- Travel to France for leaders and 14 young people £1,000
- Coach hire for the week £2,000
- Magazines and sweets for the journey £20
- Films for camera £20
- Self-catering accommodation £1,500
- Suntan cream £10
- Activity clothes needed by young people £500
- Travel insurance £1,000
- Food for the week £600
- Staff time £1,000

Notice that in bottom-up budgeting we deal with the details and try to leave no stone unturned in building up the final cost. We may of course be forced to conclude eventually that camping in Great Yarmouth has much to commend it! Some projects do finish at the feasibility stage.

Bottom-up budgeting is clearly the better method, but it is more time consuming and sometimes there is not the time available to allow for the luxury of bottom-up budgeting. On other occasions the detailed information that is necessary for this method just does not exist so a more global (top-down) approach has to suffice.

The more experienced you are in a particular field the easier it will be for you to do top-down budgeting. When you are working in an unfamiliar area then bottom-up budgeting is recommended. In either case the golden rule is to not make guesses unless they are absolutely necessary. There is nearly always someone you can go to for advice. Do not be too proud to admit that you need help in preparing the budget, and perhaps you need an additional person on your project team.

A template for most bottom-up budgets is shown in Figure 7.2.

Figure 7.2: Sample document for budgeting

	£	£
Labour	X	
Material	X	
Other	X	
Total Basic Cost		X
Add: Project Overheads	X	
Total Project Cost		X
Add: Local Overheads	X	
Add: Group Overheads	X	
Total Company/Organisation Project Cost		X
Profit (if appropriate)	X	
Initial Price		X
Add: Contingency	X	
Final Price		X

First put in your labour costs. Then insert your materials costs. You may have other costs, such as advertising, transport, accommodation. It depends on the assignment. Adding these gives the basic project cost.

In a few cases there will be a project overhead cost that is attributable to the project. Some project managers choose to distinguish between project costs and project overheads but for most projects it is acceptable to list as a cost anything that has to be done/spent in order to deliver the project.

Having completed the project costs, now add any overheads that need to be recovered. You may be managing a project for another department. The department will have calculated that its standing charges or overheads such as buildings, staff salaries, maintenance, etc is £'X' per year. They will have also assumed that they will do an estimated amount of paid work for clients in the year. Based on this, each £1.00 of cost must bear a burden or overhead and this will have been calculated as a percentage, about 20% is a guide but this can vary. So, using the percentage, it is now possible to calculate the overhead and add it to the list. If there is a further overhead charge in addition to the departmental overhead, such as organisation overhead, say 5%, then this too can be added. You now have a total cost for the project.

For non profit-making organisations that is as far as you need to go. If you work in a commercial environment then you now need to deal with the profit element.

In the same way that the finance department will have calculated its overheads it will have also calculated what it wants to earn as a percentage profit after it has recovered its costs. Using this percentage the cost to the client can be calculated. Sometimes organisations hide their profit within their overhead charges. This is not good practice. The overheads are intended to show the cost incurred in running the organisation – costs that must be recovered. Once these are included in a project budget build-up the real cost of the project will have been established. Then it is up to the organisation to decide whether or not it wishes to make a profit on its activities. If it does these can be calculated and shown separately.

Once any contingency costs are added we then have the final price for the work. However, when a contingency is put in place as part of a project the associated cost is a 'might be' cost and is not built in to the main project cost. It is added to the cost sheet at the end under the heading contingency. The money is specifically for one contingency only. It is not a buffer for any eventuality. When a point is reached in the project where the risk moment has passed, that is, the risk did not become an issue, and then the money is taken out of the contingency fund. In effect it becomes project profit – money not spent being the same as profit.

Beware of so-called contingency that is hidden in estimated timings and costs. Some people, when estimating, always add on a 'just-in-case' element as a safety precaution. The problem is that the 'just-in-case' element is not declared so it cannot be discussed and evaluated and there is no chance to make a decision as to whether to leave it in or take it out. In other words, it cannot be risk managed. And as the 'just in case' element is not declared, each subsequent viewer of the document may add their own 'just in case' element. In this kind of scenario we get so-called contingency added to contingency, added to even more contingency. Sometimes the project costs are so inflated in this hidden way that the eventual cost figure results in a tender for work being lost or an application for funding being turned down.

 Contingency costs in a project must be specific, listed, justified and signed off.

Budgeting must not be thought of as an isolated activity. It is an integral part of the plan. It needs to be continually reviewed and if necessary amended. It is closely linked with risk management and change management which are covered in the next chapter.

Preparing a simple budget exercise

This exercise has been deliberately set quite simply as it is a budgeting exercise. Many things have been excluded such as mobile telephone, use of escorts, etc., but these can be added if desired.

Imagine you decide to set up a taxi business mainly to carry disabled children to and from school, respite centres and hospitals. You will drive the taxi, your husband/wife/spouse/partner will help with the accounts and taking bookings.

You will buy a vehicle to use as the taxi and you plan to replace it every two years. You must tax the vehicle, insure it, maintain it (services and tyres) and of course you will need to put fuel in it. You will need to have a telephone for the business and you decide to have a lock-up garage in which to keep the taxi when not in use. Also there will be some miscellaneous expenses, cards, advertising, and so on. You plan to work the taxi 30,000 miles per year and you estimate that you will be carrying a paying passenger two thirds of the time you are working.

Work out your budget. Keep it simple, just estimate costs and income based on the above and then work out your gross income. Then calculate what you will charge passengers per mile. If you are really keen you might work out your break-even point, i.e. the number of passenger miles you need to do in order to recover your basic costs and start making a profit.

→

Suggested answer

Suppose you pay £18,000 for a car and sell it for £14,000 after two years, it will have cost you £2,000 per year. A lock up garage might cost you £500 per year. You will pay car tax and your insurance is likely to be £1,200. Telephone costs are estimated at £1,200. Miscellaneous items, say £500 per year. These are your 'fixed' costs. They will be incurred regardless of the amount of business that you do.

To be pedantic the telephone costs are partly 'fixed' i.e. the standing charge – and partly 'variable' i.e. the call charges which are likely to vary in proportion to the amount of work that you do. However, for this exercise we will treat them as fixed costs – accountants call this 'taking a view'.

The variable costs concern the running costs. Clearly, the more miles you do the more your running costs will increase. As you plan to do 30,000 miles you are likely to spend, in a year, £3,000 on fuel assuming you get 8 miles per litre (approx 40 miles per gallon) and pay 80p per litre (£4 per gallon).

Four tyres should do 30,000 miles so you will need a new set every year. A replacement set might cost £250. Car servicing, say two per year, could cost £1,000. Our budget – which does not include contingency for repairing dents now looks like this:

Car costs	2,000
Insurance	1,200
Lock-up	500
Tax	165
Telephone	1,200
Miscellaneous	500
Total fixed costs	5,565
Fuel	3,000
Maintenance	1,000
Tyres	250
Total variable costs	4,250
Total annual costs	9,815
Annual income based on 20,000 miles @ £1.20 /mile	24,000
Gross profit i.e. income	14,185

So there you have a simple budget.

The question is, is the business feasible or viable? Is £1.20 a fair rate? Will people use your taxi if you charge that rate? Could you charge more? What is the going rate for taxis in your area? Can you and your partner survive on the income the business generates? Are the assumptions reasonable and how accurate are the estimated costs? What changes to the budget can we reasonably make to reduce costs and increase income?

Chapter 8
The Planning Stage: Risk and Issue Management

 An issue is anything that is affecting the smooth running of the project. A risk is an issue that has not yet occurred.

The importance of risk and issue management

Without risk management there is no project management. At the start of any project and throughout the life of the project risks must be constantly anticipated and managed. New risks and issues will emerge during the life of the project and these will need to be addressed. Some risks will cease to be risks as time passes, in other words, a point will be reached where, if the event was to have occurred, it would have happened by now and these old risks can be forgotten.

Risk and issue management is ongoing throughout the life of any well- managed project.

What is Risk Management?

- Risk management is about anticipation.
- Risk management is the process of anticipating likely risks to the project and making appropriate plans to ensure that the risks do not become issues.
- Risk management involves the identifying and recording of risks, highlighting the consequences and then identifying appropriate management actions – leading to the control of the risks should they occur.
- Risk management is a balance of judgement.
- Risk management is an integral part of project management.
- Risk management is subjective – what is 'risky' to one person is 'no problem' to another.

 Successful project managers do not take risks – they manage risks.

The risk management process

- Identify risks and risk owners.
- Assess risks – the impact of the risk and the likelihood of it occurring.
- Create an Action Plan and reduce risks –- take corrective action.
- Monitor and Review risks – update throughout project life.
- Feedback on success and failures – learn from mistakes.

Risk assessment

Risk assessment is the process whereby issues are anticipated and eliminated **before** they can occur. In the perfect project a risk assessment is done and is done so well that every eventuality is anticipated and either eliminated or planned for – in other words, no issues ensue. In practice, because circumstances change throughout the life of a project, there will be a combination of issues and risks that will need to be managed.

The method for managing both issues and risks is the same. Risks and issues are:
- identified
- logged
- assessed
- resolved
- acted upon
- monitored

One way of looking at this is shown below.

Figure 8.1: Risk assessment

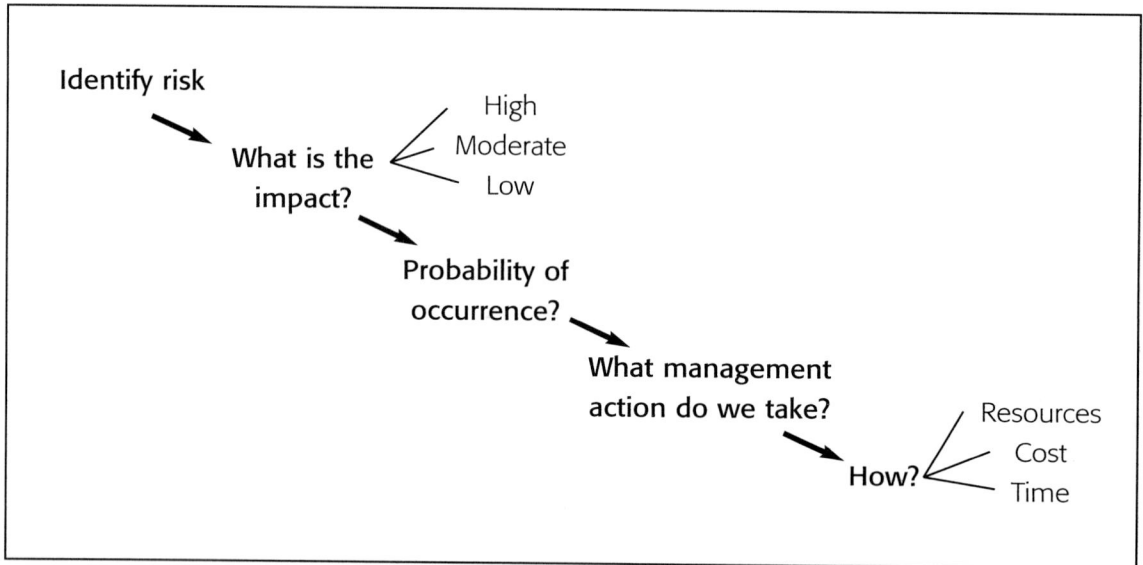

Capturing issues and risks

Project issues and risks will arise in various forms throughout the project, and it is important that the manner in which they are handled is consistent. The first element of issue and risk management concerns capturing the issues and risks and recording them. This allows for future reference and makes it easy to assess progress. Responsibility for ensuring that all captured issues are logged lies with the project manager.

The process of capturing a project issue will trigger the next stage which is to carry out an analysis before deciding on a course of action.

This analysis of each project issue should include assembling all available and relevant information including its effect on:

- costs
- timescale
- quality
- achievement of project deliverables

Identifying risks

Risks can and will be identified throughout the course of a project. The earlier a risk is identified the better. The best way to identify risks is to call a meeting involving the project team and other key players in the project. At the meeting the issue of project risks is considered, brainstorming can be used if appropriate and a list of risks is compiled. An excellent tool for this activity is the cause and effect diagram described later in this book. During the project new risks will also surface at review meetings. In child care for example, risks to children are assessed – their environment, contact with parents, monitored supervision, considering the risks of placing the children together, and so on; for the staff, for example, the environment is considered with issues of lone working, difficult clients, personal stress levels, closure and other associated risks.

Types of risk

There are three main types of risk:

- business risk
- risk to the schedule
- technical risk

Business risks include:

- Financial risk – overspending, increased inflation.
- Risk to reputation/credibility of the organisation.
- Risk to the long term customer/client relationship.
- Competitive position risk.
- Legal risks, such as copyright or patent infringement, product liability.

Risks to the schedule include:

- Shortage of resources.
- Incorrect estimates of activity times.
- Delays caused by other projects running late.
- Dependency on third parties.
- Variation requests.
- Delay in gaining approvals.
- Safety issues

Technical risks include:

- Lack of sufficient information for planning.
- Poor requirement/specification.
- Using untried technology or methodology (new IT systems, for example)
- Inadequate project solution.
- Inadequate testing.
- Under-qualified or under-motivated personnel.
- Underestimated tasks.
- Inadequate variation control.
- Inadequate documentation.

Each of these risk areas must be assessed at the start of the project and monitored at every subsequent project review stage. The list of risks is called the risk register.

The three areas of risk need to be first analysed and evaluated separately. Then, as they are all interrelated and may impact on one another, they need to be analysed and evaluated collectively.

For each risk there will be a risk owner. It will most probably be one of the project team members. It may be the project manager, but beware, remember the project manager is managing the project and the team should be managing the individual deliverables. The risk owner might be a third party, a supplier for example, and in some situations it can be the client.

Assessing risks

A risk is the combination of the effect of any action or outcome multiplied by the probability of the action or outcome occurring.

We all know that the chance of surviving an aeroplane crash is extremely low but using statistics, or working on the 'it won't happen to me ' principle we assess the likelihood of it happening as being extremely low. On the one hand we have the risk of almost certain death if there is a crash but this is offset by a belief that the chance of it happening is millions to one. So we fly, or do we? Most people fly. They make a decision to take the risk. Others, a small number it is true, choose not to fly and make other plans, in some cases choosing to forego trips they would otherwise have made.

It is all about how you assess the risk in the first place and this can be based on facts or on feelings. It also depends on your attitude to risk. Some people are naturally inclined to take risks (risk aggressive or yellow hat) and some people are caution personified (risk averse or black hat).

Although for major projects there are some sophisticated risk assessment techniques, all that is required for most projects is an assessment of each risk as to whether it is high, medium or low. Many organisations will provide guidelines or have produced statistics of various types of risk although deciding on the risk for a new situation will require judgement based on all known information. Having done this we can make some decisions as to what actions, if any, we will take. Normally, low risks are ignored. Often the medium risks are taken. The high risks, however, must be listed and for each risk a counter measure is agreed. The counter measure can be a course of action, even a change to the project plan that will eliminate or reduce the risk sufficiently for it to become one that can be taken.

A useful technique for assessing risks is as follows, where, for each risk we consider three things.

- **Impact:** how seriously the project will be affected by the event if it occurs – grade your assessment on a 1-5 scale – 1 for low impact, 5 for high impact.

- **Likelihood:** what is the chance of the event occurring – grade your assessment on a 1-5 scale – 1 for low chance of occurrence, 5 for high chance of occurrence.

- **Detection (or Preventability):** what is the chance of detecting the event sufficiently far enough in advance to stop it occurring, grade your assessment on a 1-5 scale – 1 if easy to detect, 5 if difficult to detect.

Set your results out in a table in this way:

Figure 8.2: Risk evaluation log

Risk evaluation log				
Risk	Rankings			Ranked score
	1 = unimportant 5 = serious	1 = rare 5 = frequent	1 = easy 5 = very hard	
Description	Impact (A)	Likelihood (B)	Detection (C)	(A)x(B)x(C)

Risk assessment exercise

Consider the scenario below and the risks shown. Assess them using the above method.

A celebration has been arranged at a prestigious but very small venue. The idea is that a buffet for 60 guests will be served on the lawn. The event is in August in the UK. There is very little room inside the venue so good weather is essential.

You begin to compile a risk register:

Risk	Impact	Likelihood	Detection	Score
The chief guest fails to turn up				
There is heavy rain				
The guests get food poisoning				

Only three risks are shown here, you could add further risks. Stop when you have 20.

Here is a possible result, but remember there is no correct answer. Risk assessment is a matter of judgement. It is subjective not objective. Any two groups of people given any scenario will, in all probability, come up with different risk assessments. In fact it is a good idea when doing risk assessment to split your team into two groups, do the assessment and then discuss the results.

Risk	Impact	Likelihood	Detection	Score
The chief guest fails to turn up	5	1	5	25
There is heavy rain	4	3	5	60
The guests get food poisoning	4	2	5	40

In the above assessment the logic for risk one is that without a chief guest there can be no true celebration, hence a 5 for impact. The chance of a guest not turning up is thought to be very low, hence a 1. The chance of detecting a 'no show' far enough in advance to take some action is thought to be very low and therefore high risk, hence a 5. We then multiply the figures giving an answer of 25.

The logic for risk two is that rain will not prevent the event from taking place so it cannot score 5. However, heavy rain will definitely spoil an outdoor buffet and hence spoil a special day so it gets 4. (You may argue differently. You may say that the objective for the day is to have a celebration and that anything else is of little importance. On that basis you can score the risk at 1. It all depends on what your success criteria are for the day.) The chance of detection far enough in advance to be able to take effective action is low, hence 5, so, we have a final value of 4 x 3 x 5 = 60.

For food poisoning, the logic is similar. The event will have gone ahead so not a 5. However if the guests get food poisoning the day will be remembered for the wrong reasons hence a 4. The next judgement is that you have a greater chance of getting rained on than you do of getting food poisoning hence a 2. Finally there is no chance of detection in advance hence a 5, giving a final figure of 40. We now have our risks assessed on a scale running from 1 to 125.

Risk 1 assessed at 25 is low so we will take the risk. Risk 3 assessed at 40 is low-ish so we may elect to take the risk or we could take some counter measure such as eliminating certain foods such as prawns from the menu in order to minimise the risk. If we do this the project plan (the menu) changes, so might the budget, and the assessment of likelihood will be reduced from 2 to 1.

Risk 2 assessed at 60 is pretty high on the scale, a little higher and it could be considered as a certainty rather than as a risk. We should not take the risk. Therefore we need to revisit the project plan and look for an alternative. We can change the venue or we can hire a marquee or we can issue everyone with an umbrella! The choice is yours. Whatever you choose, the project plan must be changed and the changes must be recorded and signed off by the project board.

Risk responses

When dealing with a risk we can:

- Remove the risk.
- Reduce the risk.
- Avoid the risk.
- Accept the risk.

Review risks – update throughout project life

Throughout the life of the project, the risk register should be constantly reviewed and updated. Some risks are more likely to occur in the first phase of a project, later there may be concern with the technical risks involved in designing a workable solution. Also some risks will cease to exist after a certain point in the project has been passed and new risks will crop up as the project progresses. It is therefore important to assess and review risks throughout the project.

Feedback on success and failures – learn from mistakes

As part of the risk review processes it is a good idea to make notes and discuss successes and failures, especially the ones that have incurred or avoided significant delays or costs. Reference to this file at regular intervals should help avoid the same mistakes being repeated.

In many walks of life incorrect estimates occur regularly for tasks that are done on a regular basis; journey times is one obvious example. How can we assess journey times wrongly so consistently? Is it because we are reluctant to remember or recognise previous mistakes or is it that we are stupid – or is that the same thing?

Mitigation, contingency and insurance

Mitigation

Earlier in this chapter we looked at a scenario where we were considering altering a menu in order to reduce the risk of food poisoning. This is called 'mitigation'; taking action, changing the project plan and cost in advance in order to reduce a risk. When a risk is mitigated the project cost, and sometimes the project timings, change, often for the worse.

When a risk is mitigated the costs incurred are added to the project budget and the final planned cost figure is amended. Any costs incurred as a result of mitigation can be termed as 'will be' costs, that is, costs that will be incurred. They are part of the project, unlike contingency costs which are 'might be' costs.

Mitigation is not the same as 'Contingency'.

Contingency

A contingency is where a plan is put in place in case something happens. Contingencies do not always result in costs being incurred. The paper bags that are issued to all passengers on aeroplanes are a good example of a contingency. If the flight is bumpy and the bag is used a cost is incurred which can be attributed to that specific flight. If the flight is smooth no cost is incurred and the bag is left unused and available to another passenger on another flight. Although not a very nice topic it does demonstrate the difference between mitigation and contingency.

Insurance

Insurance is not the same as Contingency. Insurance is action taken to ease or eliminate any financial loss if something specific occurs. Insurance does not stop the specific event from occurring. Taking out insurance – however sensible and worthwhile, does not have any effect in terms of reducing or eliminating risks. Having household insurance does not mitigate against a burglary – having an enormous, hungry, and unfriendly dog does!

Risk sharing – open book

By having risks clearly logged and by having any mitigation or contingency clearly logged and costed, it paves the way for risk sharing and/or open book trading. Open book trading is where the costs of the project are available for scrutiny by the client.

The premise is that the project deliverer has nothing to hide including the level of profit they plan to make on the project and that the client is sufficiently sensible to recognise that the project deliverer is entitled to make a profit.

Once this situation is reached it is possible to go 'open book' and show the client how the project has been costed. Then it is possible to consider risk sharing.

 Risk management example

Imagine you are having a conservatory built on the back of the local older person's home. You ask the builder to go over the quotation with you and in it you see the sum of £1000 for 1 metre-deep footings. You also see in the contingency section a further sum of £500 with a note added explaining that the builder believes there is a chance or risk of the local building inspector insisting that the footings are 1.5 metres or even 2 metres deep.

The builder has added the £500 at the end of the quotation together with the explanation. He has not included it in the main part of the project cost build up and he has not added a profit margin to the figure. This is the best way to do this. He could have doubled the cost in the main part of the quotation, using the flawed 'just in case' principle, but this would not stand up to scrutiny if challenged and could therefore make the builder appear dishonest.

The builder explains that the proposal is that you pay the £500 as part of the price for the job. If the footings are as planned he will make an extra £500 profit. If the footings have to be another 0.5 metres deep he will break even. If the footings have to be 2 metres deep he will be £500 out of pocket and so on.

The builder is taking all the risk. If you are not happy about this, you and the builder can agree that the final price is reduced by £500. Then if any additional costs are incurred in connection with the depth of the footings you will pay the bill for all of the additional work. In other words you 'own the risk'.

Another option is to share the risk, agree that any additional costs in connection with footings will be shared. Of course whatever you agree must be documented as part of the contract – and recorded in the appropriate place in the project file.

Create an Action Plan

An extract from another example of a risk management exercise, based around running a Summer School for young people and using a different technique, is shown below. It is well laid out showing each risk and the way it is to be managed.

See Figure 8.3.

Figure 8.3: Higher Education Summer Schools – risk assessment

Activity	Associated Risk	Management of Risk
Coach Travel to and from Summer School	• Accident en route	• Use reputable coach companies, ensure coaches have seatbelts, brief student helpers on emergency procedures
	• Participant goes missing during comfort stop or at handover between university and parents	• Facilitators to check students on and off buses • Issue guidance to facilitators about procedures (wait 30 minutes, speak to services about possible tannoy message, after further 30 minutes, phone police) • Summer School office to ring parents of any 'no shows' to check reason
	• Parents fail to materialise to pick up participant	• Facilitators to be given a list of home telephone numbers for participants. • If facilitators unable to make contact with parents, procedure should be for two facilitators to accompany the student home
	• Participant misses return coach	• Arrangements to be made by Summer School office for two student facilitators to accompany student home
	• Vandalism of coach company property	• Clear indication in Joining instructions that student will be expected to pay for any damage caused • University insurance policy
	• Substance abuse or misconduct during journey	• Clear instructions to facilitator to call police (facilitators to be provided with mobile phones)
Train Travel to and from Summer School	• Accident en route	• Beyond our control
	• Participant goes missing during unescorted phase of journey	• Ensure that Joining instructions make it clear that this phase of the journey is unescorted and that handover point is on collection from London • Block of reserved seats for all participants travelling by train • Summer School office to contact parents of any no-shows
Employer and other visits	• Accident en route to employer visits	• Use reputable coach companies, ensure coaches have seatbelts, brief student helpers on emergency procedures
	• Participant goes missing en route to employer visits	• Facilitators to check students on and off buses • Issue guidance to facilitators about procedures (wait 30 minutes, speak to services about possible tannoy message, after further 30 minutes, phone police) →

Activity	Associated Risk	Management of Risk
Employer and other visits – *contd.*	• Participant misses outward or return coach	• Facilitators to check students on and off buses • Issue guidance to facilitators about procedures (wait 30 minutes, speak to services about possible tannoy message, after further 30 minutes, phone police)
	• Fire during employer visit	• Employers to be asked to ensure that visitors are briefed on procedures on arrival
	• Hazards specific to the nature of the activity observed (e.g incidents associated with industrial machinery, chemicals etc)	• Employers to be asked to ensure that visitors are briefed on procedures on arrival
	• Incident related to unauthorised access to restricted area or unauthorised use of equipment	• Employers to be asked to ensure that visitors are briefed on arrival and are escorted at all times during visit
	• Accident or injury linked to inappropriate dress for the activity concerned.	• Careers Service to check on any specific dress requirements with employers; ensure that any participants affected by this are informed day before visit • Student helpers to be asked to check dress of those involved on boarding buses
	• Student gets lost on employer premises	• Employers to be asked to ensure visitors are given a clear meeting point on arrival • Registers on buses before departure
	• Student taken ill during visit	• Standard emergency procedures apply. Student facilitators to investigate unaccountable absences • 24 hour emergency number available to student facilitators
	• Fire	• Ensure that student facilitators are briefed on university procedures • When on non-university premises, follow local instructions
General	• Child protection	• Police checks for all staff and students who will be working in small groups or in individual contact with participants • Child protection policy

95

Risk management exercise

Consider the risks shown from two perspectives:

• Do you agree with the way the risks are to be managed?

• Identify which actions are contingency, insurance, mitigation, taking the risk etc.

Comment on the exercise

Looking at the summer school example, if a participant misses a return coach, they will be taken home by two student facilitators. This is a contingency. Why two student facilitators? Is this in order to manage another risk – almost certainly?

An accident en route is a risk that is considered to be 'beyond our control' and therefore is a risk that will be taken.

The risk of vandalism to coach company property has been mitigated (weakly) by issuing a warning that is unlikely to deter a vandal, so in effect the risk is being accepted. All that is in place is insurance.

When students are visiting industrial premises 'Hazards specific to the nature of the activity observed (e.g. incidents associated with industrial machinery, chemicals etc)' are to be managed by asking the companies to ensure that visitors are briefed on procedures on arrival. This sounds fair enough but is this a 'shared risk' or is it a risk that has now been given away and forgotten about? And what other options are there? What else can the organisers do?

Suppose your child went on this trip and had an accident. Would you blame the company where the accident occurred? Or, would you be asking questions of the organiser on the grounds that they were ultimately responsible for your child's safety? If you were then shown the risk log above would you be happy that the organisers had done all it could?

What is certain is that there would be no doubt that the organiser had procedures in place and had made a professional attempt to manage the risk.

Risk management summary

• Risk management is not an optional extra that you use to improve your project.

• Without risk management there is no effective project management.

• Risk management is used throughout the life of the project.

• Mitigation is action taken to ensure that something specific does not occur.

• Contingency is a plan that is in place should something specific occur.

• Insurance does not stop the specific event from occurring.

• Project managers do not take risks – they manage risks.

Chapter 9
The Delivery Stage: Controlling the Project

The project manager is responsible for ensuring that the appropriate levels of control are in place and that control information is up-to-date and known by the appropriate people. The key to successful project reporting and control lies to a great extent in the way that risks and changes to scope are managed.

Project control

Controlling a project involves monitoring, controlling and reporting on all of the following:

- risks
- changes to scope
- time
- cost
- quality
- personnel issues

Controlling risks

We have mentioned elsewhere the importance of managing risks as an on-going exercise throughout the life of a project. The same importance must be assigned to changes of scope – for which the change control procedures exist.

Controlling changes to scope – Change Control

Change control is the management process that tracks and documents all changes to the scope of the project.

In the perfect project there is no need for change control. The project objectives will be clear and will never change; the success criteria and deliverables will be specified and will not change; there will be no issues and/or risks that have not been foreseen and planned for; there will be no change of mind; nothing will be overlooked in the planning; the sun will shine every day and we shall live happily ever after … But projects are imperfect. Things will be overlooked by everyone. Objectives and deliverables agreed and signed off at the start of the project may be found to require modification as time passes. Oversights in the planning will be discovered and new risks will appear. The customer may have a change of mind. The goalposts **will** move.

Why bother with change control?

By having a change control process in place we can ensure that at all times we know exactly where the goalposts are; why the goalposts are where they are; who agreed that they should be there; who is responsible for them being there and if any costs or delays to the project have been incurred who is responsible for them:

- Change control makes it possible for a project to be audited.
- Change control ensures that when the project manager's performance is evaluated any delays or increased costs introduced as a result of 'goalposts moving' are not held against the project manager.
- Change control ensures that the project objectives and success criteria and deliverables and timings and costs are always current and agreed.
- Change control keeps projects on track.
- Change control ensures that the responsibility for costs, both financial and other, and delays due to goalpost moving are fairly and squarely apportioned to the appropriate people.

Without change control there is no project control.

At this point you may be thinking that this is all very well but that you are not working on multi-million pound projects. You may even be thinking that in fact you rarely see any information about costs on your projects. Even if this is the case, all of the principles of change control will still apply on your projects. Change control is not just about money. Change control procedures will allow you to track **any changes** to the project scope.

If change controls are in place and used they will:

- Promote effective team communication.
- Improve the decision making process by establishing the guidelines for implementing changes and assessing their impact
- Help the project manager to manage changes and schedule resources effectively.
- Make visible changes of scope, responsibilities, and the associated impact on schedule and costs.
- Keep track of requirements.

The change control process

During a project, many questions, issues and suggestions are encountered culminating in requests for change. Change requests can affect:

- operations
- equipment requirements
- deliverables
- cost
- timings

Any change in customer/client requirements identified after the agreement of the contract, i.e. the project definition and success criteria, is a change of scope and must be documented and signed off.

Remember that what some people might consider trivial may be of huge significance to you and vice versa. What might seem to be a small deviation from plan to you may have a 'knock on' effect or 'ripple effect' elsewhere that could be crucial.

Recognising changes is not always easy since changes are not always overtly requested. It may be that the project manager will need to identify work to be performed that is outside the original scope, or is not costed. This underlines the importance of the project manager knowing the detail of the project, i.e. the 'scope'. The project manager should contact the relevant people without delay, preferably before the extra work is done, to request that it be formally added to the project scope. It is essential that this agreement is recorded.

All changes to the scope of a project should be raised at a project control meeting and eventually signed off by the project board.

This does not mean that the project manager cannot go ahead with the work. The project manager can take the decision to proceed with the work, in advance of approval, but must be sure that approval will be given. The decision will be influenced by the project manager's knowledge of the projects key success criteria and by the cost of the work involved. He or she must be sure of their own scope. If in doubt they should contact the sponsor but if this is necessary, it does indicate some failings during the project definition stage.

To summarise:
- Change management is the tool that will ensure that if the 'goalposts are moved' then it will be done in a controlled way.
- Change management will prevent a project from losing its way.
- Without change management there is no effective project management.

The project file

All control information plus any other documentation about the project should be kept by the project manager in a project file. The file should contain an up-to-date written record of all actions, events, contacts with the customer and sub-contractors, and information relevant to project planning.

Keeping separate notebooks is a dangerous practice but sometimes it is not practical to carry project files around. When separate notebooks are used it is vital that the information is transferred into the main file on a frequent and regular basis. It may be that the budget will support the purchase of a personal organiser or laptop?

The project file must be in sufficient detail to allow another person to take over the planning and/or running of the project in the event of illness, an accident or the unexpected departure of the project manager.

Project control information

Project control information will come from two main sources:

- What you are told at review meetings.
- What you see as you 'walk the job'.

Holding review meetings

In theory, review meetings should only be held when necessary, the implication being that having to set a date is wrong. However, bearing in mind that people need to organise their time it is often sensible to have a set date for review meetings. Also there is a theory that meetings can be more efficient if people do not have to attend for the whole meeting and that they just attend for the items that concern them. This is fine if you can do it.

However, it is often the case that information that is thought to be of no interest to a particular person, or discipline, turns out to be very significant. One idea – or gimmick? – is to hold meetings with the participants standing up. The thinking behind it is to reduce the time spent on the meeting.

The over-riding principle in managing a successful project review meeting is to avoid participants, and/or affected parties from feeling that they are being overlooked or not party to decision making or dissemination of information and not being in the picture.

The review meeting agenda

The agenda should be the same as for the original project definition meeting. All items should be re-visited:

- The project's aims and objectives – to verify that they have not changed.
- The success criteria – to verify that they are un-changed and that they are on schedule. In practice you are likely to find that a change of scope will require the project success criteria to be amended or that a failure to deliver will mean that a target date or cost or performance criterion is under threat.
- Roles and responsibilities will pick up team changes and issues.
- Project risks – some new risks may have been thought of which might affect the project timing or the project budget. Some existing risks may now be obsolete because the point when they might have occurred has passed. These can be removed from the risk register.

When you have been through this agenda you will have checked on every aspect of the project and will have the data necessary to put together the minutes of the meeting plus any reports that need issuing.

The meeting minutes

Keep the meeting minutes simple. All you need to record is the **actions** that are to be taken as a result of the meeting. Use a simple format:

Action   who   when   notes

A successful meeting should leave behind it a trail of clear crisp decisions.

Chairing meetings is not an easy job so consider using an outsider to chair the meeting, someone who is not in any way affected by the project outcome. They will be in a very strong position to chair any meeting impartially.

From time to time, issue a questionnaire at the end of a meeting asking the delegates to comment on the quality of the meeting to show that you are trying to do things correctly. You may also unearth a difficulty before it becomes a major issue.

At your review meeting you will be told the progress of individual elements of the project by the person(s) responsible for delivering that element. Most of what you are told will be true, but there may be some things that are incorrect, some honest wrong beliefs, and some, a very small percentage, will be misinformation or downright 'fibs'.

Initially the project manager's approach should be to take the information on face value – unless there is good reason to be doubtful. You will soon discover the people who are unreliable and you can then decide how to deal with them.

Walking the job

You will get the rest of your information by 'walking the job'. Walking the job means exactly what it says. Get out amongst the staff, chat to them, see how they look, listen to what they say, be very aware of what they don't say, note their body language. As a result of all that you hear and what you see, and don't see, you will have a pretty good idea of progress. You will then be able to predict the information that you will get at any review meeting.

Monitoring and controlling the timing

A simple way to monitor and control a project is to use a milestone chart i.e. a chart showing just the key points in the life of the project. The milestones can then be coloured in red, green or amber to denote the current state of progress:

- Green indicates that all is well and that the milestone has been or is expected to be met on time.
- Amber indicates that there is cause for concern – usually an amber marking is accompanied by a note indicating some corrective action and who is to take the action.
- Red indicates that the milestone will be, or has been, missed. Again, this will be accompanied by a reference indicating what the expected date now is.

This system is sometimes called a RAG (red, amber, green) system, or the traffic light system. It is ideal for reporting to people who only need to know the overall picture – the project board for example. Another example might be when an office move is taking place, office staff need to know what is happening but may not need a lot of detail.

For people who need the detail e.g. the project team members who are delivering a part of the project, an amended form of Work Breakdown Schedule can be used.

Taking the original WBS as a template we can add any columns we wish, depending on what we wish to report. Figure 9.1 is an example. In it we have chosen to report on timings, costs and on cash flow. For the timings we show the original or planned forecast completion date and in the next column we show the latest forecast completion date. When the two show a variance or discrepancy it is usual to add an explanatory note. The same principle applies to costs and to cash flow. (Note – Cash flow is not dealt with in this book but is a key element in major projects.). See Figure 9.1.

The information that appears in this document comes from knowledge gained during day-to-day 'walkabouts', plus information gathered at regular progress or review meetings. Clearly the most important activities are those that are on the critical path since if these are late the project will be late. However, delay on any activity can be crucial as following activities may be disrupted by their lateness. It is important to monitor **all** activities.

If any critical activities are subject to delay this will be reflected in the most important figure of all, namely, the latest forecast completion date for the completed project. Let us assume that we are 4 weeks (i.e. 20 working days) into a project and several activities should have been completed. Most are non-critical – i.e. there is some 'float'- and one is a critical activity. The critical activity was planned to take 4 weeks but is now expected to be 2 days late. The completion date for the whole project was 30 weeks. What do we now forecast as the latest forecast completion date? Is it 30 weeks, on the assumption that we will catch up lost ground? Or is it 30 weeks plus 2 days, on the assumption that there will be no other delays. Or do we assume that as we are currently 10% late (2 day's slippage in 20 days) the whole project is likely to be 10% late and hence will finish in week 33?

The truest way to report this situation is to assume that the project will be 10% late – i.e. take the worst case scenario.

Monitoring and controlling the costs

The simplest way to monitor and control costs is shown. Put in the planned cost and then the 'latest forecast cost at completion'. Where there is a difference add an explanatory note.

 Example

Item	Planned cost	Latest final cost at completion (FCAC)	Comments
Recruit staff	£10k	£11k	see note 12
Supply phones etc.	£4k	£3.5k	see note 3
Total cost	£92k	£96k	

Figure 9.1: WBS example

Activity No.	Activity	Costs (£)		Cash Flow (£) To Date		Completion Dates	
		Estimate	Latest Forecast or Actual	Estimate	Actual	Estimate	Latest Forecast or Actual
01	Set Out	200	180	200	180	Day 2	Day 2
02	Foundations	1800	1900	1800	1900	Day 8	Day 7
03	Ground Floor Drains	900	850	900	850	Day 5	Day 5
04	Ground Floor Slab	1200	1250	1200	1250	Day 11	Day 10
05	Walls	10000	9000	1500	2000	Day 33	Day 31
06	Roof	1000	1000			Day 36	Day 35
07	Joinery	3000	3000			Day 37	Day 36
08	Electrics	1600	1600			Day 35	Day 34
09	Plumbing	3000	3000			Day 37	Day 36
10	Glazing	200	200			Day 38	Day 37
11	Building Weathertight	-	-			Day 38	Day 37
12	Plastering	2500	2500			Day 48	Day 47
13	Decoration	2400	2400			Day 56	Day 55
14	Clean and Tidy Site	400	400			Day 60	Day 59
15	House Complete	-	-			Day 60	Day 59
	Overheads	6000	5900	1400	1400	-	-
	TOTAL	34200	33180	7000	7580		

The principle of forecasting the final cost at completion is the same as that for forecasting dates. If the only activity completed to date is 10% overspent then assume that the project as a whole will be 10% overspent.

The techniques above are usually sufficient for small projects or projects of short duration. However on longer or larger projects slightly more sophisticated techniques might be appropriate to track, control and report information.

A slightly more complex way of presenting progress data is to have a column showing the variance from plan.

 Example

Item	Planned cost	Latest FCAC	Variance	Comments
Recruit staff	£10k	£11k	(£1k)	increased advertising costs
Supply phones etc.	£4k	£3.5k	£0.5k	BT price reduction
Total cost	£92k	£96k	(£4k)	

The key figure here is the total cost and the variance (£4k) – these are the figures the project board will want to see. Unless the variance is considered to be significant, further details will not be required.

Imagine a project where the original planned cost was, say, £30k but then the government has a change of mind and reduces their requirements – thus reducing the budget by £2k. The change of scope is agreed and noted using the change control procedure. At the same time, another activity in the project is found to have been incorrectly estimated and is now going to go £5k over budget.

How do we report this? Compared to the original forecast the project is £3k above target. However, the original planned cost has changed by agreement so in this case the true measure of the project manager's performance should be against the revised planned figure.

A simple way to manage this is to have additional columns on the report so that we can show the original planned cost, the revised planned cost reduced by £2k following changes in directive and the latest forecast cost at completion increased by £5k.

 Example

Planned	Revised Planned Cost	Forecast FCAC	Variance	Index	Comments
£30k	£28k	£33k	£5k		£2k scope change
					£5k overspend

Note here that the variance and the measure of the project's, and hence the project manager's, performance is against the revised planned cost not the original cost. Note also that the £5k overspend does not figure in the revised cost column as it is **not** a revised cost but is an overspend.

Reporting in this way makes it easy to see that the original estimate for the project (£30k) has changed — but in a controlled way — i.e. the projects financial deliverable (target) is now £28k. It also shows that the new planned cost is likely to be overspent by £5k as a result of poor project management.

 Example

A very experienced project manager said that, in his younger days, he had in his project reporting deliberately 'lost' or 'hidden' £2m. Not easy to do but he did it. There was no sinister motive. It was just a precaution in case something went wrong in the £27m project. Eventually, when he was sure that it was safe to do so, he unveiled the extra £2m profit at one of the regular monthly project reporting meetings. He expected to be congratulated on his skilful handling of the budget. Instead the project board came very close to sacking him. They had bosses too and knew that they would have to explain the extra £2m and how it was that a junior project manager could hide it without them knowing.

Monitoring and controlling the quality/performance

Project quality is usually to do with two things:

- Specification — meaning the materials, personnel, data and equipment used either in the finished (delivered) service or in the delivery process.

- Performance — meaning the functions that the delivered solution can perform or the conditions that exist as a result of the project being delivered.

If the project definition report says that the project will be staffed by senior people, each equipped with a laptop computer then that is the specification or contract. If it was agreed that they will be given access to certain restricted information, by a certain date, and in a specific format then that is the specification. Any deviations from the specification or contract are quality issues that need reporting and addressing.

Use the change documentation to raise these issues. If the delivered solution is meant to reduce complaints by 10% this is measurable and can be reported. If the delivered solution is meant to increase the number of telephone calls made by a call centre in a day, this is measurable and can be reported. If the service intervals at a day centre are meant to increase from every 6 weeks to every 12 weeks this is measurable and so on.

Most quality measurements involve a practical, pre-determined test or an assessment by an independent expert identified at the start of the project.

Example: the importance of taking corrective action

An experienced management consultant was invited to team up with another consultant, with whom she had previously not worked, to help him to present a series of courses. On the evening before the first course he produced a timed running sheet together with a set of documents all in chronological order. The running sheet was very detailed and very specific:

09.00	Course introduction	Russell	Documents
09.03	Delegates interviews	Sheila	
09.08	Feedback from interviews	Sheila	
09.18	Exercise – 'Motivation'	Russell	Doc 1

and so on...

Sheila was impressed by the level of detail and somewhat in awe of the professionalism of the preparation. She just hoped she would not let Russell down. On the first day of the course Sheila could see that they were falling behind schedule, so at around 11am she asked Russell 'How are we doing?' 'We are 20 minutes adrift' he replied.

'So what do we do?' Sheila asked.

'Well,' he said, 'Are you in a hurry to get away tonight?'

'I suppose not', Sheila replied.

That night the course finished at 6pm against the targeted finish of 5pm. This pattern continued for the remainder of the three-day course, a late finish every evening.

By the second course Russell and Sheila were on good professional terms. The second course started to run late. Sheila asked Russell how they were doing and they went through the same routine ending with him suggesting that they work late. Sheila's face must have told a story, because he asked if she had a problem with working late.

'Working late is not an issue, but working later than we planned to is', she said. 'It makes us look unprofessional and it is not fair on the delegates – our customers – as they expect us to work to the agreed programme. Some of them will have made plans based around a published finish time. Why do you have these detailed plans if we can't keep to them?'

'Well', Russell replied, 'They show me how far adrift we are'.

'But that is only of use if we then do something about it', Sheila responded'. 'I can't produce training plans as professionally as you do, but I can finish on time. We need to cut something out of the course so that we can get back on schedule'.

'What do you suggest?' asked Russell.

They went through the course, re-prioritised the sessions, decided on the 'musts' as opposed to the 'nice to's' and from then on finished at 5pm. The delegates went away happy as Russell and Sheila had not invaded their time and had came across as professional presenters.

The above might also be usefully considered in the context of the chapter on team building, particularly relating to the part on forming, storming, norming and performing.

Personnel issues

Part of project control concerns personnel issues. Under this heading we address any changes to the composition of the team. Also we address any team issues that may come to light. What is **not** addressed here is 'poor performance' of any individual. Review meetings are not the place to embarrass people in front of their peers.

If, elsewhere in the meeting, it has become apparent that an individual is consistently failing to deliver their element of the project the focus will have been on the positive actions needed to recover the situation.

Poor performance of individuals is clearly unacceptable and it is the project manager's job to deal with it swiftly. It needs to be done outside of any review meeting. Initially it will be a one-to-one conversation between the project manager and the person in order to establish the causes of the poor performance. Remember, it is a problem that needs a solution, so it is a mini-project and step one is to establish the real nature of the problem before jumping to conclusions. If this does not solve the problem, the personnel manager may need to be involved. Whatever the solution – a change of performance or a change of personnel – there must be a solution.

Reporting to the project board

The project board should only need a very basic report giving an indication of whether timing, costs and performance are to plan. An example is shown below:

Figure 9.2: Project control report

Project Title: House Number 1
Report Period: Day 14
Date of Report: 1.2.95

Item	Estimate	Latest Forecast or Actual
Total Cost	£34,200	£33,180
Cash Flow to Date	£7,000	£7,500
Completion Date	Day 60	Day 59
Quality	Foundations completed satisfactorily. Brickwork standard acceptable.	

The project board will only need detail if the project manager fails to show clearly that the project is on course. Even with a project that is slipping, the project board may be satisfied with minimal detail so long as the project manager shows that corrective action is in place for each slippage. In other words, if the project board can see that you are managing the project and that you are aware of the details and are doing something about it, it is likely that they will leave you alone. It is a question of whether or not they have confidence in you.

There will be projects where the project manager will be expected to make a face-to-face presentation to the project board at regular intervals to let them know how things are progressing.

When preparing for these meetings, a good tip is to remember the 4/40 technique used when reporting on multi-million pound projects. The 4/40 technique involves preparing 40 slides, four containing the key information, the rest containing supporting data. The idea is that you will anticipate all the likely questions that you will need answers to and you will address these issues on the four slides. Preparing the four slides is a mini project of course, because you must get your objectives and success criteria, the answers, clear and then deliver them convincingly. If you do this you will satisfy the project board and you will not need to use the other slides. Should you be asked a question that is not adequately covered on the main slides you can then use the back-up slides to deliver the answer. Depending on the size of your project you can scale the technique down to suit the project you are working on. A 1/10 ratio will be adequate for most projects.

A project manager said that he once reported to the project board that his project was still 'on plan' and that very little that was untoward had happened since he last reported. It had been, he said, 'A very dull month'.

His boss relied, 'Tim, I like dull projects. Try to keep all your projects dull, dull, and dull'.

The soft option

There are times when, as project manager, you will feel alone. You will want to speak to your sponsor face-to-face so that you know they have received your message and so that you have had an opportunity to gauge their reaction – something that you can not do using emails.

Your sponsor may be busy and hard to pin down or may be only partially committed to the project and as a result is keeping out of the way. You must not let this prevent you from having the face-to-face meeting so try the SOFT option. It works this way.

Put together a one or two minute summary describing the following key elements concerning your project:

- **S**uccesses
- **O**pportunities
- **F**ailures
- **T**hreats

Then, all you have to do is to decide when and where to intercept your target. If you know they come to work by train then bump into them at the station and walk the 200 yards to work with them giving them the update as you do. It can all be done quite casually and you can get some idea of the impact or response that the news generates. Or, bump into them in the lunch queue or at the sandwich bar that they use. The point is you need to ensure that, interested or not, they have the appropriate information and that you have been able to gauge their reaction. Follow up with an email by all means but make sure that you speak to them first.

Project closure

Eventually your review meeting will lead you to one of two conclusions:

- That the project should be aborted.
- That the project is completed.

Projects can be aborted for many reasons. Sometimes the conditions for aborting the project will have been set at the start of the project – i.e. as well as success criteria, failure criteria will have been established. Mostly projects are aborted when it becomes clear that one of the three main criteria, time, money or quality are not going to be met and the project board is unwilling to change the project scope to overcome the deficiency.

The other scenario occurs when, as you go through the review meeting agenda, you find that:

- The project objectives have been met.
- The success criteria have been met.
- The risk log is empty.
- All changes to scope are resolved and all monies are paid or collected.

When you reach this point you know the project is concluded. The minutes of the final review meeting become the minutes of the project closure meeting and the report becomes the project closure report. The project manager's key activities at the closure of a major project are:

- Updating administrative systems and the project file to show that the project has been closed.
- Archiving relevant material.
- Updating any reference databases with learning from the project, positive and negative.
- Identifying any follow-on opportunities.
- Producing a formal record of assessment on project personnel performance.
- Identifying any training/retraining requirements for team members.
- Arranging re-deployment of team members if appropriate.
- Disposing of project assets.
- Providing feedback to the quality and safety system.

Your project is now completed and only one thing remains. After the dust has settled – usually between six weeks and six months – hold a post project review meeting.

Post project review

Make sure that the actions resulting from the project closure meeting have been attended to satisfactorily. The bullet points shown above can be used as your success criteria for the meeting. Make sure that the post-project review meeting dwells on the successful aspects of the project as well as the less successful aspects. The project is over. Learn from it and make plans to avoid the not so good bits next time.

In summary

When reporting on projects the golden rules are:

- Only report the amount of detail that is required.
- Always report the worst case scenario.
- Report any bad news as soon as possible.
- Don't tell fibs.
- Try to have **dull** projects.
- Formally close the project.
- Hold a post project review meeting.

Remember

If the project went well and you were the project manager make sure your team gets the recognition it deserves – and make sure **you** do too!

Section 3

Management Tools and Techniques

Chapter 10
Selecting the Project Team

The importance of team selection

Earlier, we stressed the importance of team selection. Successful project managers use their persuasive skills to ensure that they get the right project team around them. They know that to embark on a project with a group of people that have neither the expertise, the motivation or the blend of personal attributes necessary for success is tantamount to 'planning to fail'.

A frequently raised issue on training courses is 'We are given the project team – we have no say in its composition'. Whilst recognising that in the real world project teams are often put together using the 'who's available?' or 'who can we get?' or even 'are there any volunteers?' approach – this does not make it right.

The project manager must have a say in project team composition. Unless the project manager is happy that the assembled team is suitable for the project in hand the project manager should not proceed. It is difficult enough to manage projects, even with a good team. Accepting a project where the team given is unsuitable is a recipe for failure. You should try to have the team changed or you should not accept the project.

If you are serious about a project and seriously want it to be successful – then it is essential to give team selection careful thought. The better your team selection the less motivational and leadership work you will be required to perform.

Techniques to aid team selection

Techniques to aid team selection include the work done by Isabel Briggs Meyers and Katherine Briggs who developed a Personality Style Profile. This is a highly thought-of technique used by many international organisations as an integral part of their recruitment and selection process. The technique involves the subject completing a questionnaire that leads in turn to the discovery of which of sixteen possible profiles applies to the subject. Also, which of four basic temperaments applies? Armed with this information it is possible to be more scientific in team selection. (see *Introduction to Type* – Myers and Briggs).

Charles Handy developed a simple questionnaire that categorises people as 'Strategists', 'Carers' and 'Fighters' and armed with this information it is possible to ensure that there is not too much imbalance in any proposed team. (see *Understanding Organisations* – Handy).

Edward de Bono developed a concept of 'Thinking Hats' and using this simple concept can help to ensure that a balanced team is put together. (see *Six Thinking Hats* – De Bono).

Psychometric testing, another widely used and generally well thought of technique gives an indication, in general terms, of the kind of work to which the subject will be most suited. (See *Modern Psychometrics* by Rust and Golombok). There is also a self-assessment test on the web (Psychometrics.com). Specifically aimed at teams and behaviour within teams is the work of Meredith Belbin. He studied teams in action and in his original thesis listed eight team types and their likely behaviour in any team. Belbin's work is well regarded by many organisations and is widely used as a routine part of the recruitment process. Belbin's theory is that all eight team types are necessary for a team to be successful. Also there are no 'stars' and no 'bit players'. All are as valuable as the next. Belbin's descriptions of the team types and likely behaviour also include allowable weaknesses, so a rounded picture 'warts and all' can be ascertained when considering putting certain individuals into a team. (see *Management Teams and Why they Succeed or Fail* – Belbin).

All the above techniques can be of value and further information about them can be obtained in the relevant books.

Do these techniques work? It is possible to select people with certain skills and abilities and it is possible to build balanced teams. It is not easy though and requires determination and the ability to modify or re-assess both your methods and your criteria.

Ensuring successful team performance

For successful team performance it is essential to ensure that:

- The team members are competent in the appropriate disciplines for the project.

- The team members are able to work together especially when problems are encountered.

- There is an effective, agreed method for resolving issues.

- The team members are formally assigned to the team.

- Team performance is reviewed regularly.

All team members must be competent in the discipline that they are bringing to the project. This does not mean they need to be an expert. Nor does it mean they have to be the best available. They must be adequate, acceptable, and good enough. If they are not good enough they should not be in the team. But, being 'good enough' is not the same as being the best or even the best available. Many project teams fail because they are made up from 'the best available'. It is better to have a person in the team that will fit in rather than have an expert who will disrupt things.

Whatever the discipline, if a technical or operational problem arises that is outside your experience, you can always get help from associates, colleagues, your boss or your professional association. However, when problems occur that are behaviour related it is extremely difficult to solve them.

For the team members to be able to work together when problems are encountered it is important to have the right mix. This does not mean having a group of people who don't argue and have mild disagreements because this often means getting on at the expense of getting things done. What is needed is a mix that will be capable of dealing with a variety of situations, including their own disagreements, resolving them and acting cohesively upon them. Much work has been done to take the guesswork out of team selection, all of it based on predicting the behaviour of people.

An effective method for resolving issues, agreed in advance, ensures that when a difficult moment arrives there will be no need to waste valuable time in deciding how to reach agreement. Decisions can be reached using straight numerical voting i.e. six in favour, five against, means proposal is accepted. Chair (usually the project manager) to have the casting vote in the event of a tie.

Consensus might be the agreed method, i.e. instead of voting, the proposal must be one that all parties – even though not agreeing with every element, are prepared to agree to and support. In government this is called collective cabinet responsibility. In essence it means that if you cannot agree to support the proposed course of action then you should resign. What you cannot do, when consensus is the agreed method, is reluctantly agree at the decision making meeting, then by your actions, inaction or comments, show that you really disagreed with the decision taken.

It may be that the agreed method is that after a full and frank discussion the project manager will decide on the course of action to be taken. Many people favour this method as the project manager is ultimately accountable. Benign dictatorship is the name for this method!

 The method for making decisions is less important than having agreed – in advance – what the method is.

Team members should be formally assigned to the team even when they are only part-time on the team. This makes it quite clear to all concerned that the project is important, and that it is not a minor activity that will be fitted in as and when possible. It also confronts the 'I'm doing you a favour' attitude that might prevail if the person concerned is not formally assigned to the project.

'Teams that operate without reviewing performance may get really good at doing things badly'.

Team performance should be reviewed regularly bearing in mind the above.

Earlier on the issue of volunteers was mentioned. Volunteers are sometimes not good news for project managers. There is a world famous voluntary organisation in the UK that uses many volunteers. Most of their projects are late and much of the lateness is caused by volunteers not turning up to do the work promised on the agreed dates or just not being up

115

to the tasks they have been asked to perform.. The advice is to use volunteers sparingly if possible but always train them and treat them with respect as you would any other member of the team.

Summary

Putting a team together without giving the matter considerable thought is inviting disaster. For those people who do not have the resources to be able to call on or use special techniques, the bottom line of all the above is this:

*   Teams containing all the best, most senior or most experienced people nearly always fail. It is often better to have a relatively junior person in the team rather than a more senior or more experienced person who is difficult to work with.
*   Teams are not meant to get on swimmingly all the time.
*   Conflict is not necessarily a bad thing. Most successful teams have conflict, but they work through it, make a joint decision and then go forward together.
*   Do not be afraid to have a 'prickly' person in the team.
*   It is better for teams to be 'good on the ground' rather than good on paper.

Maintaining effective team effort

The project manager is responsible for ensuring that the project team is motivated and that there is nothing stopping them from doing a good job. If the project manager is regularly having to do work that was assigned to others – then something is wrong.

When people are not motivated they resort to using 'get out of jail' cards, similar to those used in the game of Monopoly. A 'get out of jail card' might be 'nobody told me!' or 'I thought you were doing that' or 'my boss gave me an urgent job to do' just to mention three. The project manager's job is to ensure that the existence of these 'cards' is kept to a minimum.

Some people see the project manager's role as being at the top of the management triangle, issuing instructions and overseeing that the work gets done, as below.

project manager

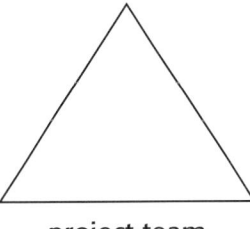

Figure 11.1   project team

From a motivational point of view it might be better to look at it this way, with the project manager supporting the team making sure that there is nothing to prevent the team from performing.

project team

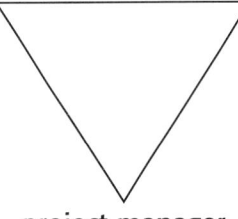

Figure 11.2   project manager

This can be done by trying to ensure that everything that the team needs is in place and of the appropriate standard. Make sure that:

- Satisfactory accommodation is provided.
- Equipment is readily available and easily accessed.
- Team procedures are clearly understood and easy to follow.
- Communication between the project team members and the project manager is swift and open.
- Decisions are made promptly.
- Information is shared promptly between project team members and project manager.
- Progress meetings are held to up-date people formally.
- Issues are resolved rapidly.
- High quality work is recognised.
- Satisfactory work is recognised.

Project team behaviour

All teams must deal with four essential issues:

- Clarifying their mission, goals and objectives.
- Defining roles and responsibilities.
- Working out procedures.
- Managing the interpersonal relationships.

A newly formed team will follow a well-recognised path to the point where they are operating well. The stages of development are:

Forming

During this phase team members do not really know each other well and are concerned with how they will fit in and who the leader is. At this time the nominated leader must provide strong leadership and direction otherwise informal leaders may well take over and misdirect the team. During the forming stage people are likely to be on their best behaviour, trying to fit in, not making waves. All might seem to be going well – but do not assume that it will last.

Storming

During this stage of the team's development, the members may well start to question their goals, their direction and the leadership. This may be quite frustrating. Best behaviour will give way to normal beahviour and even bad behaviour. Unless team members can be objective and mature many teams do not pass beyond this stage. The leader must work closely with the team during this stage.

Norming

This is the stage where team members begin to resolve their differences, develop unwritten rules and begin to feel more comfortable working together. Each team member has learnt what to expect of each other and their relative position in the team. Leadership needs to be participative at this time.

Performing

This is the stage where leadership is less important as team members develop a sense of success based on teamwork with a quality output. Team members will often enjoy working together at this stage, and the leader is unlikely to need to intervene even if the team is experiencing a difficulty.

We established earlier that in most projects the three key criteria, time, money and quality will be monitored on a regular basis as part of the agreed project control procedure. Less likely to be monitored are the way that the team is performing and the way the team feels about its performance. Often people fall into the trap of thinking that because the project is on track then the team must be happy. If you want to check that the team is feeling OK about the project and the way the team is functioning then use a simple questionnaire such as the one shown here.

Review – group effectiveness questionnaire
Put a circle around the figure that best meets your view

How well do we plan the project?
Comment

very well				badly
5	4	3	2	1

How well do we make use of time?
Comment

very well				badly
5	4	3	2	1

How well do we communicate with each other?
Comment

very well				badly
5	4	3	2	1

How effective are we in handling disagreements or conflicts?
Comment

very well				not at all effective
5	4	3	2	1

How committed are you personally to the outcome of the project?
Comment

very well				not at all committed
5	4	3	2	1

Overall, how well do we work as a team on this project?
Comment

very well				badly
5	4	3	2	1

From time to time ask the team to complete and collate the results. That way, if there are any issues that need addressing, you will get advanced warning. If the questionnaires show that all is well and then suddenly out of the blue a team member raises an issue that they have been keeping to themselves for some time, then you can, in your defence, point out that you have tried to anticipate problems. You will, of course still have to deal with the issue but the point will have been made that you are trying to run an 'open' management regime, by use of regular review.

Motivation, leadership and interventions

Many thousands of words have been written on the subjects of motivation, leadership and the problems of intervention i.e. when to intervene and when to stay on the sidelines. Here we will try to identify some of the key outcomes from all of this work.

Motivation

People expect to be dealt with in a way that always maintains or enhances their self-esteem. Anything that knocks a person's self-esteem will cause them to either drop their heads or get angry. In either event productivity falls away as they concentrate on their own feelings rather than on the job in hand.

Make a list of 'de-motivators' – i.e. all the things that you think might cause a person to drop their head or get cross. On training courses groups have come up with as many as 60 as Figure 11.3 shows.

Figure 11.3: Some de-motivators

• Lack of consultation	• Job status	• Jealously
• Lack of reward	• Rudeness	• Removal of overtime
• Being ignored	• Drunkenness	• Lack of discipline
• Lack of recognition	• Rumour	• Fear
• Health	• Safety	• In wrong job
• The work itself	• External interference	• Distractions
• Lack of time	• Family	• Familiarity
• Overwork	• Taxation	• Broken promises
• Stress	• Reversal of decisions	• Not belonging
• The telephone	• Red tape	• Denial of resources
• Meetings	• Distortion	• Favouritism
• Laziness in others	• Lack of equality	• Pomposity
• Rules	• Too much control	• Poor promotion prospects
• Lack of authority	• No support	• Hunger
• Lack of information	• Vagueness	• Domestic problems
• Poor pay	• Putting things off	• Weather
• No objective	• Financial injustice	• Trust
• No opportunity	• Petty rules	• Lack of trust
• The workplace environment	• Lack of flexibility	• Inconsistency
• The people at work	• Overbearing manner	• No recognition
• Lack of social activity	• Secrecy	• Unjustified cost cutting
• Too little work	• Playing politics	• No training
• Policy	• Boredom	• Redundancy

From the list of de-motivators here are just a few of the most common and most powerful ones:

- Having an incompetent boss.
- Not being kept in the picture.
- Being spoken to badly.
- Being coerced or bullied or unfairly treated.
- Being unfairly paid compared to the market rate or to a colleague.

Having an incompetent boss

Bearing in mind that we have already said that a project manager cannot be technically competent in all aspects of a project, how does this tally with being a competent boss? Well, the answer is that people expect you to be competent in project management and then to be sufficiently bright enough to grasp technical concepts when they are explained to you. The first criterion is more important than the second in most cases.

Not being kept in the picture

Despite what people will say to you, such as 'I'm not bothered', 'I couldn't care less', 'it doesn't concern me' people do want to know what is going on around them. Always strive to give people as much information as possible. If in doubt give them too much information.

Being spoken to badly

No one likes this, so do not do it. When you slip up and speak to someone badly, and you will, apologise immediately. Having said that let us be clear that speaking to someone badly such as name calling or shouting at them, is not the same as letting a person see that you are angry or upset about something. It is perfectly normal behaviour for people to get angry or upset, and to show it, so long as it does not lead to abuse. As a manager you are not expected to be so in control of yourself that you come across as a 'speak your weight machine'. The reality is that bosses who occasionally show that they are human too usually have a good rapport with their colleagues. Be yourself – but be civil.

Being coerced or bullied or unfairly treated

We mentioned 'clout' earlier. Managing using clout is not recommended, even if you have it. Make your decisions and deal with people and judge their performance based on measurable, factual information. You will then be in a strong position when you come to persuade people that a particular course of action is required, whether it is a decision that needs implementing or a performance improvement that you require.

Being unfairly paid compared to the market rate or to a colleague

It is often said that money is not a motivator. It is true that money is not the prime motivator. If it were true, we would have many fewer nurses, teachers and carers. However, not being paid a fair rate for the job is a major demotivational factor. Getting less than a colleague doing similar work, or having to do more work than a colleague on similar pay, is guaranteed to cause resentment.

The project manager, as leader of the project team, is responsible for understanding the myriad of things that can cause team members to lose their motivation. We have touched on just five. At the same time the project manager is expected to attend to the equally important business of monitoring the day-to-day progress of the project. We can now see why the project manager should avoid, if possible, having further responsibility such as delivering a component of the project.

Leadership

Leaders come in all shapes and sizes and there are many styles of leadership. First and foremost, the project manager needs to be clear about his/her own preferred style, the one that is most natural to them. Then, they need to be aware of the style that is most applicable to the team as a whole, the style that suits each individual within the team and finally the style that is most appropriate for the project, or situation. These will not necessarily be the same.

So leadership is not easy. There are conflicting needs. The group needs one style of leadership, individuals need their own treatment, but the task may demand a certain style. The leader has a preferred or natural style that is determined by his/her personality or make up. There is also the leader's vision, the video playing in their head that shows the project being carried out in the preferred way. If that is not enough all of this is dependent on whether or not the leader has the authority of the group, meaning that the leader's behaviour and competence, or credibility, is such that the team will accept the leader's direction.

Beware of treating everyone the same. No two people are alike, so it is wrong to treat them alike. Try to give fair treatment to everyone. But do not treat them all the same.

'There is nothing as unequal as the equal treatment of unequals'.

The above quote is from *Leadership and the One-Minute Manager* by Kenneth Blanchard, Patricia Zigarmi and Drea Zigarmi. It explains the leadership process very well.

McGregor, in *The Professional Manager*, identified two basic leadership styles. He called them Theory 'X' and Theory 'Y'. Theory 'X' managers believe that people need to be told what to do and when to do it and need to be constantly monitored. They believe that without supervision the work will not get done. The fact is that there are some Theory 'X' people about and they do need that treatment.

Theory 'Y' managers believe that if you explain the end results that are required and any parameters that exist, a person will then be motivated to work with a minimum of supervision and will deliver the required result within the agreed parameters. There are many people in the world who wish and need to be treated in this way. If you supervise theory 'Y' people too closely they will resent it.

The key thing to be aware of is that it is important to manage people in the style that they (the people) are used to. If your natural style is theory 'Y' but you take over a group that is used to close control, your theory 'Y' style will seem to them to be one of aloofness or disinterest and their performance will fall away. Similarly a theory 'X' manager, taking over a group that is used to being left to 'deliver the goods' in their own way, will find a hostile response to any perceived interference.

So how does a leader know which style is appropriate? Is it possible to change style anyway? And how does the leader know when it is appropriate to intervene?

Interventions

On the question of intervention the best advice is to think of the way you would treat a child or young person during their formative years. When a child is very young nearly every decision is made for the child by the parent; what they eat, what they wear, what they can and cannot do. As the child grows up the parent gradually does less for the child and more and more of the decision-making is done by the child. It is a question of maturity. When the child is sufficiently mature to do the task or make the decision, then the parent does not/ should not intervene.

When dealing with adults the same principle can often be used. How mature is the person in the given situation? A managing director can feel very threatened when faced with a new IT system if no training has been given. The Head mentioned in the story at the start of this book is an extremely competent and successful person, but when dealing with a re-location project was out of her depth.

When a daughter is having her first child, should her mother give advice? The answer is 'Yes ' even though the advice may not be welcome however tactfully it is offered. The 'mum-to-be' is immature in the situation (hence the great show of knowledge and confidence) and it is right that someone with experience of the same situation should intervene even though the intervention may be unwelcome! No one said intervention was easy but sometimes it is necessary and right, regardless of the way that the intervention is received.

Obviously the greater the personal skills of the intervener the less chance there is of unwelcome feedback. It is the same in project management. The question is what are the circumstances and what is the level of maturity of the person dealing with the situation? Depending on the answers to these questions the project manager can decide whether to intervene or not.

If the project manager recognises a situation where one of the team or the whole team is struggling, then intervention (help) might be called for. Some care is required here as there are levels of maturity. So the decision is not as simple as 'intervene' or 'not intervene', there are shades of grey. Sometimes it is appropriate to continue to keep an eye on things but not intervene. Sometimes it is appropriate to offer help but to back off if help is rejected. On other occasions intervention is appropriate, welcome or not.

A husband and wife team ran a private social work agency. The husband gave his people tasks and deadlines and then left them to get on with it. The wife gave her people tasks and deadlines and then constantly checked up on them. The problem was they were both dealing with the same group of people – mature staff. He was thought of as an OK manager. Her nick-name was Miss Piggy. She only had one style of management (Theory X) and so was unable to change her style when dealing with a mature group. Find out if your team have a nick-name for you – it could tell you a lot!

Are you Bond or Blofeld?

Many project managers find themselves adopting what I call the James Bond approach to project management – thinking on ones feet, always in the thick of things, avoiding disaster at the last minute, whilst leaving a trail of destruction behind, and, eventually prevailing over the villain and arch planner Blofeld. But the truth of the matter is that had Blofeld and Bond been real people – Blofeld would have won – hands down!

There is a saying: *'If you don't like the heat – stay out of the kitchen'.* Do not accept a project management role until you have considered all the implications, including your own strengths and weaknesses, especially the question of how you will cope when the pressure is on.

Chapter 12
Some Problem Solving Tools

In a way problem solving is a misnomer because the biggest part of problem solving is problem definition. So, many of the techniques that follow are as much about problem definition and data collection as they are about problem solving.

The thinking process

Before looking at problem solving techniques we need to consider some factors that have a major bearing on the outcome of any problem solving session. The first is our attitude to the thinking process. Some people have difficulty distinguishing between facts, opinions, theories, and honest wrong beliefs. These people do not make good problem solvers and may be known as 'lazy' thinkers.

Facts

We need to remember that a fact is something that we have observed ourselves or that has been observed by others and can be verified. All fact and factual statements relate to the past, not to the future. Facts are evidence based and supported by data in some form.

Opinions

Opinions often give a clue to the way people feel about an idea or proposal. Opinions are important and need to be considered, so long as they are not confused with facts.

Theories

Theories are really assumptions that a particular cause will give a certain effect. Many people are convinced that showing violence on TV results in increased violence in our daily lives, yet we are told that there is no evidence to prove this theory.

Honest wrong beliefs

We all have certain ideas put into our heads as we grow up, the intention being to equip us better to live in the particular culture in which we are born. Some of us believe that it is wrong to steal; others honestly believe that if people are daft enough to leave their things unattended then it is only sensible to take them.

As we go through life we add to our collection of honestly held, but often misguided, beliefs. Some examples might include:

- Metal is always stronger than plastic.
- When a husband and wife split up the children should always go with the mother.
- People of another race or religion do not think the same way as us.

When examining potential solutions to problems, honest wrong beliefs can be a big stumbling block. They can occur in any situation and often cannot be refuted by logic.

There are many problem solving techniques available to the project manager. The ones that follow are the most simple and easiest to use.

Concentration diagrams

Concentration diagrams work on the principle that a picture is worth a thousand words. They are used when there is a need to record both the frequency and the location of an occurrence. A drawing is made of the item or area in question and a mark is made on the drawing at the spot where the defect/situation that is being monitored occurred.

Examples of where they can be used:
- Location of defects – e.g. rust spots on a car.
- Occurrences of child abuse within a neighbourhood.
- Where a batsman scores his runs.
- Location of older people who are likely to require services.
- Accident black spots on the roads or in a building.

Figure 12.1: Juvenile disturbance 'hotspots' map

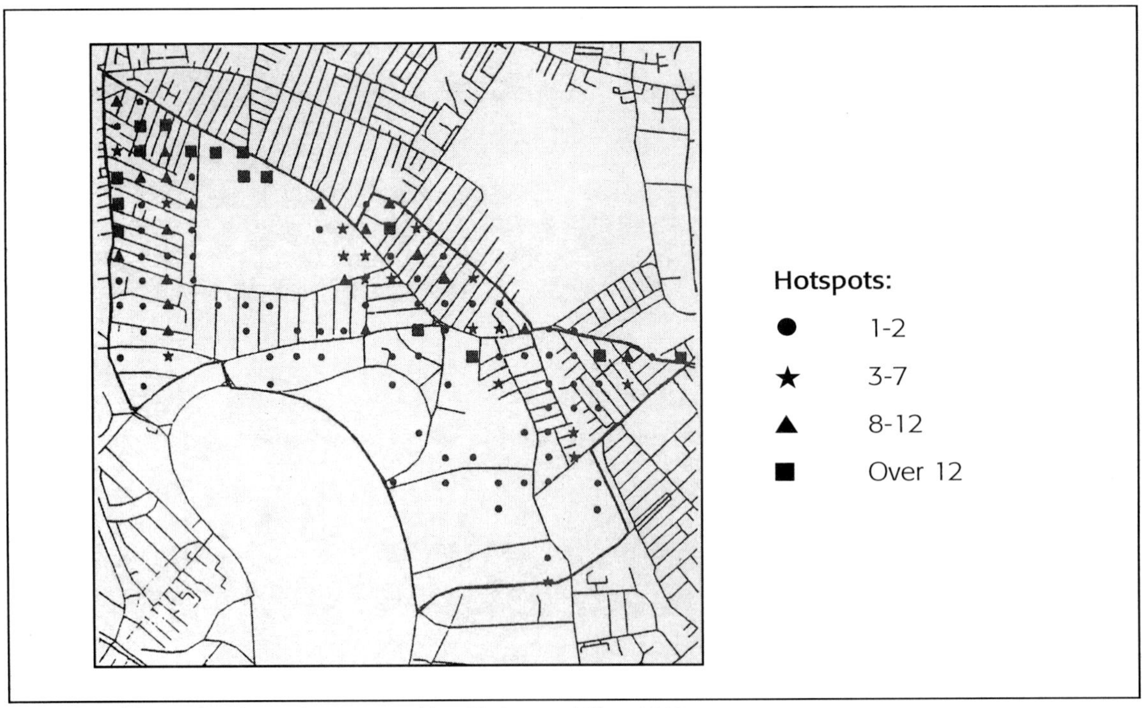

Reproduced from *Planning Safer Communities*, Marlow and Pitts, 1998

Concentration diagrams in action

Examples of concentration diagrams would include the ones that show clusters of leukaemia cases adjacent to nuclear waste processing plants, or more recently, the instances of cancer clustered around the locations of mobile phone masts. **Beware** – it may be necessary to keep the diagrams confidential or to prepare them in such a way so that the exact location cannot be recognised. In this way the identity of the people concerned cannot be easily identified.

When preparing to collect data using a concentration diagram, the steps you need to follow are:

- Decide data required and the parameters of the data that is needed.
- Design a concentration diagram.
- Test the diagram by asking someone to use it.
- Collect data.

Cause and effect diagrams (C&E)

A cause and effect diagram, also known as a Fishbone or Ishikawa diagram, is an effective way of recording data and making it easy to see relationships between possible causes and the end effect. It might also be used to organise brainstorming sessions. They look like this:

Figure 12.2: Cause and effect diagram (C&E)

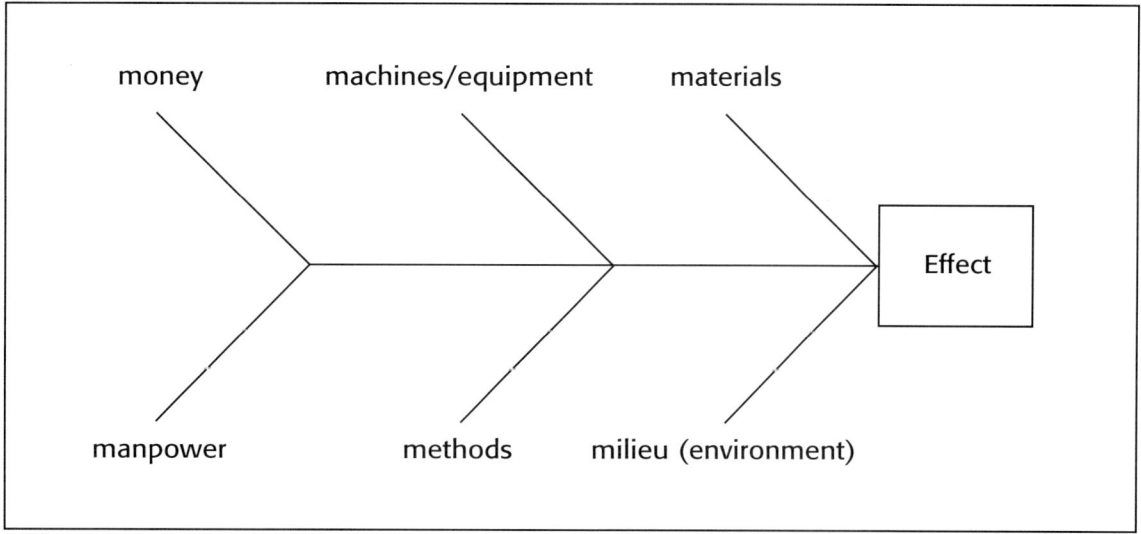

The diagrams are constructed in three stages:

Stage 1
Establish what the problem or effect is – start the diagram by putting this in a box.

Stage 2
Attempt to identify possible major causes – put these on the branches of the fishbone. An easy way to label the branches on a fishbone is to use the six 'M's, namely:

- materials
- manpower
- methods
- money
- machines and equipment
- milieu

The illustration shows how this is done. If it is more appropriate, however, feel free to label the main branches with other suitable headings.

Stage 3

Look for any subdivisions of the major causes. It may be useful to list all possible causes first and then put them on to the diagram. Do not exclude a possible cause because you think it does not apply in the particular case you are considering. The diagram is meant to show all possible causes. That way it will be a permanent trouble-shooting tool that can be used whenever a similar situation arises.

If a particular cause has a large number (say more than 20) of sub-causes, it is useful to turn it into a separate diagram. To focus discussion, circle the most likely causes and draw lines to indicate the relationship between them.

Building the diagram

Usually the diagram is built with one person writing in phrases on the diagram and a team contributing their ideas. The beauty of the technique is the concise and visual way in which contributing causes can be documented on one diagram. It requires literally minutes of instruction in order for any person to understand it. It is important when constructing a C&A diagram to remember that all potential causes are being logged.

Sometimes there is doubt as to whether a cause should be put under one branch or another. Put it under the most likely branch or even both. What is important is that it has been thought about and recorded, rather than where it sits.

Building a C&A diagram gives several potential benefits:

- It can help to prevent a group from jumping to a hasty conclusion.
- By plotting all potential causes you create a trouble shooting tool for all future occasions when you are faced with the same or similar problem.
- When you are trying to motivate a group for example it is a good idea to start off the diagram with the group and then leave it with them, for a week or so, time permitting, so that they can add things to it. It is a good way of inviting 'buy-in' and the quantity and quality of the additions to the chart are a very good indication of the amount of interest or 'buy-in' you are generating.

Look out for, and examine closely, the relationships between causes. This is where unexpected solutions are likely to arise. If you start to become overwhelmed with causes, you have not defined the problem efficiently. Remember, the aim is not to solve the problem at this stage, nor to apportion blame, but to understand the problem well enough to propose solutions.

Follow the above ground rules to ensure the technique works effectively, and use large diagrams, people will participate if they can see what is going on.

A variation on the basic diagram is the 'CEDAC' diagram. CEDAC stands for 'cause and effect diagram with additional cards'.

It is the same Ishikawa diagram except that cards (Post-it notes are ideal) containing notes and ideas (possible solutions) on each particular cause are attached to the diagram. This addition is very useful because it allows elaboration on the thinking. The diagram can be kept on display and as further information or thoughts are acquired more 'Post-it's' are added to the diagram.

When you have completed your cause and effect diagram, the next step is to consider each of the possible causes to see if there is information to show that it is a factor in the case that you are investigating.

Collecting evidence

Evidence comes from many sources:

- government statistics
- research
- the organisation's records

Having collected the evidence you will be in a position to say which causes apply, in the case you are considering, and which do not. The important point being that any decision is evidence based. For some of the possible causes there will be no evidence. In these cases you will need to mount a mini project to collect evidence. However, remember that before doing this, the scope of the project needs to be changed to incorporate the additional work and 'sign off' must be obtained.

Managing the evidence – Pareto Analysis

Pareto Analysis is a technique for analysing information relating to a problem and displaying the results graphically. It is sometimes known as the 80/20 Rule after Count Pareto – an Italian economist who discovered that data often separates into approximately an 80/20 split.

Examples are:

- 80% of a company's sales will be to 20% of its clients.
- 80% of domestic accidents will be the result of 20% of the possible causes.
- 80% of your telephone bill will come from 20% of your calls.
- 80% of your time will be taken up by 20% of the tasks you regularly tackle.
- 80% of your shopping budget will be spent on 20% of the items purchased.
- 80% of your organisation's project budget will be spent on 20% of the projects.

The 80/20 principle does not mean that exactly 80% of the total problem is provided for by 20% of the features but that it will be approximately that proportion. The ratio itself is not as important as the fact that it is the major causes that are being identified.

Suppose a publishing company analysed its stock of books. The likelihood is that they would find that about 80% of the stock value was incurred by 20% of the 'titles', the next 15% of the stock value is incurred by a further 30% of the 'titles, and the remaining 5% of the stock value is incurred by the remaining 50% of the 'titles'. These are called the A, B and C class items.

Some organisations analyse the projects currently under way – based on the 'added value' they will generate and find a similar pattern emerges. Then it categorises its projects A, B and C in order of importance to the organisation. Armed with this information management decision-making can ensure that the levels of effort and control can be prioritised with most effort and control going on the 'A' class projects, then diminishing in intensity to the 'C' class projects.

 **Example**

The process based on a hypothetical survey into absence from school

Step 1 – List activities to be analysed and place in column 1. (See Figure 12.3.)

Step 2 – Count how often they occur and place in column 2.

Step 3 – Calculate the total for column 2 and the percentage that each item represents of this total (column 3).

Step 4 – Order totals, starting with the largest, and calculate the cumulative percentage as you go down the list.

Figure 12.3: Pareto recording results

1	2	3	4
Reason	Frequency	% of Total	Cumulative %
Overslept	48	41	41
Thought it was Sunday	35	30	71
Bus Late	18	15	86
Unwell	10	9	95
Clothes in wash	6	5	100
Total	117	100	

Already we can see from the table that the big hitters are 'overslept' and 'thought it was Sunday' – accounting for 71% of the problem. We could stop here but sometimes it is useful to get the message across by showing the data in the form of a histogram.

Step 5 – Draw the Pareto diagram by using the figures in Column 3

Figure 12.4: Pareto histogram

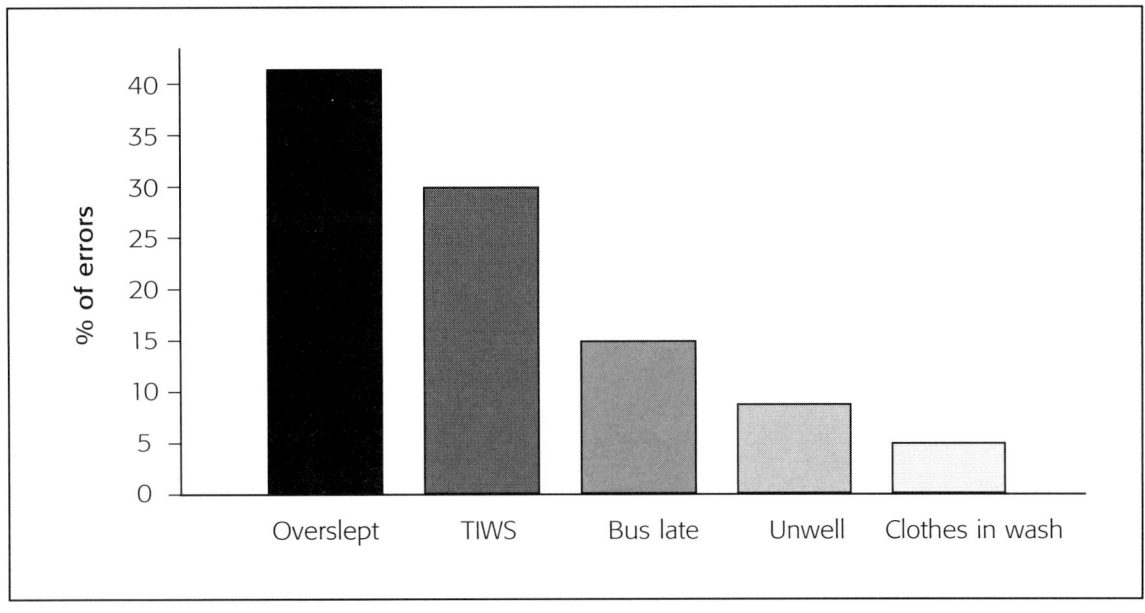

Step 6 – Interpret results.

The candidates for priority action, in this case overslept and TIWS, appear on the left of the Pareto diagram. In our example overslept and TIWS account for 71% of the problem. If we tackle these two areas and are, say 10% successful – we will have reduced the size of the problem by 7.1%. On the other hand if we addressed the issue of clothes in wash and were 100% successful we would only have reduced the size of the overall problem by 5%.

Pareto analysis directs us to the high impact areas (vital few) and helps us avoid wasting time on low impact areas (useful many). Very often the simple process of arranging data may suggest something of importance that would otherwise have gone unnoticed. Selecting classifications, tabulating data, ordering data, and constructing the Pareto diagram can serve a useful purpose in problem investigation.

Having now identified the key causes of any problem the time is right to look for feasible solutions.

Brainstorming

The brainstorming technique has a somewhat tarnished reputation in the UK as it is often interpreted as a meeting where ideas are sought, then discussed and accepted or rejected. Whilst this method of problem solving is used all too frequently – it is **not** brainstorming.

Brainstorming is the rapid pooling of all and any ideas that a group of people can come up with before any discussion or judgement takes place. Every idea is recorded. Everyone is expected to participate. The emphasis is on volume and breadth of suggestions, not on how rational they sound. Here, spontaneity is more important than considered opinion.

The purpose of the technique is to collect as many ideas as possible, as raw material for subsequent discussion. It is most useful when a problem is complex or the solution is not obvious.

Brainstorming can be a useful technique for releasing ideas, overcoming inhibitions, cross-fertilising ideas and getting away from patterned thinking. However, brainstorming sessions need to be planned and executed carefully and proper evaluation is essential.

Brainstorming – The process

Assemble a group of between six and twelve people. Most should be directly involved with the problem, but it is a good idea to draw some from other areas – even from areas that have no remote connection with the problem. This will ensure that different ideas and experience will be available to consider the problem. Appoint a chairperson and a note-taker.

The chairperson, and it does not have to be the project manager, should define the rules, emphasising that:
- The aim is to get as many ideas as possible.
- No attempt will be made to evaluate any ideas.
- No one should feel inhibited about coming up with suggestions.

Think about having a warm up session to familiarise the group with the procedure. For example, they could be asked to suggest how many uses they can think of for a paper clip.

Some rules for brainstorming meetings:
- Keep a relaxed atmosphere.
- Make your meetings disciplined but informal.
- Choose a comfortable, undisturbed venue.
- Choose a leader – The chair, or leader, checks that everyone understands how the session will operate and ensures the rules are obeyed.
- Get the right team – The technique seems to work best with groups of five to seven people – too few and there is less chance of a lively atmosphere, too many and the intensity of activity is lost.
- Define the problem clearly.
- State explicitly what it is that needs solving – make sure everyone in the group understands.
- Generate as many ideas as possible – all suggestions, provided they address the problem, and no matter how off-beat they may seem at first sight, are welcomed and accepted. Free-wheeling is encouraged.
- No discussion or evaluation – criticism and comment must be deferred – this prevents any idea being rejected before it has had a proper airing. This helps to overcome inhibitions caused by anticipation of immediate, adverse response, and it means imaginations can flow freely; there is no need for analysis of ideas before trying to articulate them.

- Give everyone equal opportunity to contribute – Everyone must have an equal chance to participate and be encouraged to use it. Ask members in turn for their ideas – a free for all is more informal but could allow one or two to dominate. Go back round the group several times, allowing the first suggestions to spark off new ones.
- Write down every idea – elect someone to record each idea as it is presented without editing. Preferably use a board so members can see the list developing.
- Allow time for ideas to incubate, perhaps brainstorm in sessions, with say a few days between them. Initially quantity is more important than quality; let ideas turn over in people's minds; suggestions may then be developed or new ones added.
- Remember that, however creative you are, what you finally decide on has to work. It has to satisfy the success criteria set out in the project definition. Brainstorming and other techniques for increasing creativity will help you to break new ground, but eventually you will have to think clearly and analytically about the pros and cons of the preferred solution before making your final decision. This is called critical examination and is dealt with later in this chapter.

We need to let unconventional ideas come forward without making any judgement on them. Sometimes the apparently wild suggestion that turns convention on its head can provide the best answer.

We must find a way of shedding inhibitions and allow creativity to flourish. Brainstorming, done properly, is a technique for achieving this. Use brainstorming selectively, where there seems to be ample scope for different ideas. It will not solve all your problems but can help you to crash through the barriers erected by the traditional approaches to decision making.

The nominal group technique (NGT)

Many people find that 'pure' brainstorming takes too much time and effort to get working properly. A few attempts, with no clear success, is usually enough to cause the process to be abandoned. As a result an alternative and sometimes more acceptable method has evolved. This is sometimes referred to as the nominal group technique. It is a very good strategy but needs at least as much preparation as brainstorming.

This technique uses both individual and group strengths, using each as appropriate, and prevents domination by particular individuals. It is a technique that can be used for issue identification, idea generation, and for almost any problem solving scenario.

First get your team together. Then explain how the procedure works. You will need a facilitator. It can be the project manager – but does not have to be. It is a good idea to let the facilitator role change around from meeting to meeting.

The meeting begins in the same way a brainstorming session does – with the facilitator reading out a statement of the problem to be tackled by the team. The statement must be carefully prepared and written out, not merely presented 'off the cuff'. After hearing the statement there may be questions seeking clarification. The facilitator should not now try to revise the problem statement but should encourage the participants to restate the problem in their own words. The facilitator may even nominate two or three members to restate the problem. This is a deliberate stage which forces the team to think through the problem statement in their own words. The facilitator must prevent any team member from dominating, and must not allow the problem to be 'hijacked'. The original problem statement written out by the facilitator is not altered; it is merely a process of restating in the team's own terms. The facilitator allows discussion to continue until problem formulation, as expressed by the team, seems satisfactory. (This process is a mini project clarification meeting – the problem solving process being a mini project).

Having clarified the problem the team then works in silence for about 15 minutes, during which time each team member writes out his or her responses, alternatives, or suggestions to the problem statement. The team should remain in one room during this time as the atmosphere of work encourages mental concentration. Team members who may finish early are still required to remain in the room without talking. The silent generation period is used because study has shown that this is the most effective initial way to generate a variety of viewpoints and ideas. The facilitator will discourage talking but may cut short the period if everyone seems to have completed the task. The facilitator should emphasise, however, that creativity has not stopped and that new ideas can be added to the team member's list at any time.

When the silent stage is over the facilitator asks each team member in turn to put forward an idea or suggestion. These will usually be taken from team member's lists but not necessarily so. When each idea is put forward, the facilitator may seek clarification from the team member, but must not change or develop the idea. Other team members are not allowed to participate in these discussions but must wait their turn.

No criticism is allowed by team members or the facilitator. As each idea is put forward and clarified it is entered onto a chart by the facilitator or assistant. Only one idea is put forward by each team member before passing onto the next member. This process continues until ideas begin to run out and team members 'pass'. When there are no more ideas the stage ends.

With all ideas entered onto charts displayed around the room, clarification can begin. The facilitator goes through each suggestion in turn. Once again criticism is not allowed, and each idea is further explained as necessary. Team members may suggest modifications or additions. The team must also group together ideas that they consider to be similar. This may result in some deletions and rephrasing. It is important that this stage stays positive and does not get bogged down in detail. The facilitator must be firm.

When all the suggestions are clarified the facilitator issues cards to each team member. Individually and in silence, each member selects the top six ideas and writes the ideas on cards together with the ranking at the top of the card. Six points goes to the most preferred idea, one point to the least preferred.

The facilitator and assistant then gather up the cards and write up the results on a new chart. Next to each idea, transferred from the cards, is written the rankings as given by all the team members. Each idea will have a string of numbers, being the rankings as given by team members. There may be several zeros, where a team member did not rank the idea in the top six. Now the scores are added up to give the final ranking. In the case of a tie, the idea having the highest number of team member rankings, as opposed to the total score, wins.

The result is a ranked set of ideas that has been generated without dominance by any team member. Even though it may not be a complete team consensus, it at least comes close to this ideal.

Now we are ready to evaluate each of the ideas so critical examination can start.

Critical examination

This is the point in the process where we take each idea and examine it to see if it will work, and if so how it will work and with what implications?

The key point to remember at this stage is to ensure that the criticism is done in a professional manner. It is vital to ensure that group members do not raise objections that are based on 'honest wrong beliefs' or on 'pre-programmed' ideas that are not evidence based. There are people who carry around in their heads many 'put down' phrases that they use on a regular basis. It saves them from thinking. The job of the facilitator at the meeting is to ensure that these 'put downs' are eliminated. One way of doing it is to issue a list at the start of the meeting – just to remind everyone what phrases to avoid. A suitable list might include the following, which was taken from a training slide:

 Example

- We tried that before.
- Our place is different.
- It costs too much.
- That's beyond our responsibility.
- We're all too busy to do that.
- That's not my job.
- It's too radical a change.
- We don't have the time.
- Not enough help.
- Our plant is too small for it.
- Not practical for these people.
- The staff will never buy it.
- The union will scream.
- It isn't in the budget.
- We've never done it before.
- It's against our policy.
- Runs up our overheads.
- We don't have the authority.
- That's too ivory tower.
- Let's get back to reality.
- That's not our problem.
- Why change it, it's still working OK.
- I don't like the idea.
- You're right...but....You're two years ahead of your time.
- We're not ready for that.
- We don't have the money.
- Can't teach old dog new tricks.
- Good thought, but impractical.
- Let's hold it in abeyance.
- I'll give it more thought.
- Top management would never go for it.
- Let's put it in writing.
- We'll be the laughing stock.
- Not that again.
- It would cost too much money in the long run.
- Where'd you dig that one up? We did all right without it.
- It's never been tried before.
- That's what we can expect from the staff.
- Let's shelve it for the time being.
- Let's form a committee.
- Has anyone else ever tried it? I don't see the connection.
- It won't work here.
- What you are really saying is...Maybe that will work in your department, but not in mine.
- Let's all sleep on it.
- The Executive Committee will never go for it.
- What do they do elsewhere? Don't you think we should look into it further before we act? It can't be done.
- It's too much trouble to change.
- It won't pay for itself.
- Know someone who tried it.
- It's impossible.
- We've always done it this way.

135

Figure 12.5: Critical examination sheet

Job title
Job output
Present method
Charted by   Date

Purpose	What is achieved?	What else could be done?
	Is it necessary? Why?	What should be done?
Means	How is it done?	How else could it be done?
	Why that way?	How should it be done?
Sequence	When is it done?	When else could it be done?
	When then?	When should it be done?
Place	Where is it done?	Where else could it be done?
	Why there?	Where should it be done?
Person	Who does it?	Who else could do it?
	Why that person?	Who should do it?
Recommendations for improvement of present method		

Critical Analysis can be done in a number of ways – but the simplest is to use Rudyard Kipling's six stalwart serving men.

> *I had six stalwart serving men;*
> *They taught me all I knew.*
> *They are the what, the where and when*
> *The why, the how and who?*
> Rudyard Kipling

By repeatedly asking the questions – **why**, **what**, **where**, **when** and **how** of the idea it will soon become apparent which ideas will be workable and which will not. To aid you in this process see the format shown in Figure 12.5.

During the critical examination some of the ideas will prove to be unworkable. Don't be afraid to brainstorm the difficulty that makes the idea unworkable. You may find a way around the difficulty and the idea may then get re-started and prove to be a winner.

Eventually you should have an idea that is workable and meets whatever success criteria you set for yourselves. Sometimes you are lucky and have more than one idea that meets the success criteria. When this happens you need to have a way of making the decision as to which one to select.

Decision matrices

Decision matrices allow you to compare alternative options in a way that takes much of the subjectivity out of the decision making process. The completed matrix provides an excellent reference document enabling the decision making process and the criteria used to be recorded for future reference.

Let us assume that you are about to purchase a new car. You obtain some quotes for suitable vehicles but are undecided which is the best buy for you.

Method 1

You list the criteria that are important to you and put a simple 'yes' or 'no' against each characteristic. This results in the chart below:

Figure 12.6: Car attribute matrix

Decision criteria	Car A	Car B	Car C
Cost range £16-18k	yes	yes	yes
Air conditioning	yes		yes
Extended warranty		yes	
12,000 mile service intervals		yes	yes
Air bags	yes		
Leather upholstery	yes	yes	yes

From this we can see that a decision will be difficult as all three cars score four 'yes's

Method 2

In Method 2 we rank the cars in each category – then allocate a point's score (arbitrarily) to each ranking mark. So car A wins on price – earning 10 points – but is joint third on extended warranty. We then add the point scores.

As you can see – using this method car A is the winner as it comes out with the lowest score:

Figure 12.7: Ranked car attribute matrix

Decision criteria	Car A	Car B	Car C
Cost range £16-18k	1(10)	2(8)	3(7)
Air conditioning	1(10)	3(5)	1(10)
Extended warranty	3(0)	1(10)	3(0)
12,000 mile service intervals	3(0)	2(7)	1(10)
Air bags	1(10)	3(0)	3(0)
Leather upholstery	2(8)	1(10)	3(7)
	11 (38)	12 (35)	14 (34)

Method 3

In Method 3, each criterion is 'weighted' following discussion and the mark for each criterion is multiplied by the weighting. When these are added we can see that car C is the clear winner.

Figure 12.8: Weighted car attribute matrix

Decision criteria	Weighting	Car A Score W T	Car B Score W T	Car C Score W T
Cost range £16-18k	10	10 x 10 = 100	10 x 8 = 80	10 x 7 = 70
Air conditioning	8	8 x 10 = 80	8 x 0 = 0	8 x 10 = 80
Extended warranty	5	5 x 0 = 0	5 x 7 = 35	5 x 0 = 0
12,000 mile service intervals	10	10 x 0 = 0	10 x 7 = 70	10 x 10 = 100
Air bags	4	4 x 10 = 40	4 x 0 = 0	4 x 0 = 0
Leather upholstery	8	8 x 8 = 64	8 x 10 = 80	8 x 7 = 56
		284	265	306

Clearly, the result is strongly influenced by the weighting. What would be the effect if '12,000 service intervals' was rated at 2 instead of 10 and 'air bags' was 10 instead of 4? See answer below:

Figure 12.9: Alternative weighted car attribute matrix

Decision criteria	Weighting	A Score W T	B Score W T	C Score W T
Cost Range £16-18k	10	10 X 10 = 100	10 X 8 = 80	10 X 7 = 70
Air conditioning	8	8 X 10 = 80	8 X 0 = 0	8 X 10 = 80
Extended warranty	5	5 X 0 = 0	5 X 7 = 35	5 X 0 = 0
12,000 mile service intervals	2	2 X 0 = 0	2 X 7 = 14	2 X 10 = 20
Air bags	10	10 X 10 = 100	10 X 0 = 0	10 X 0 = 0
Leather upholstery	8	8 X 8 = 64	8 X 10 = 80	8 X 7 = 56
		344	209	226

Flowcharting

The steps involved in creating a flowchart are:
- Decide beginning and end.
- Arrange the activities and decision points in the appropriate order, using arrows to show direction of flow. If necessary, break down the activities into simple steps to reduce their complexity.

Figure 12.10: Making a homeless application – a quick reference flowchart

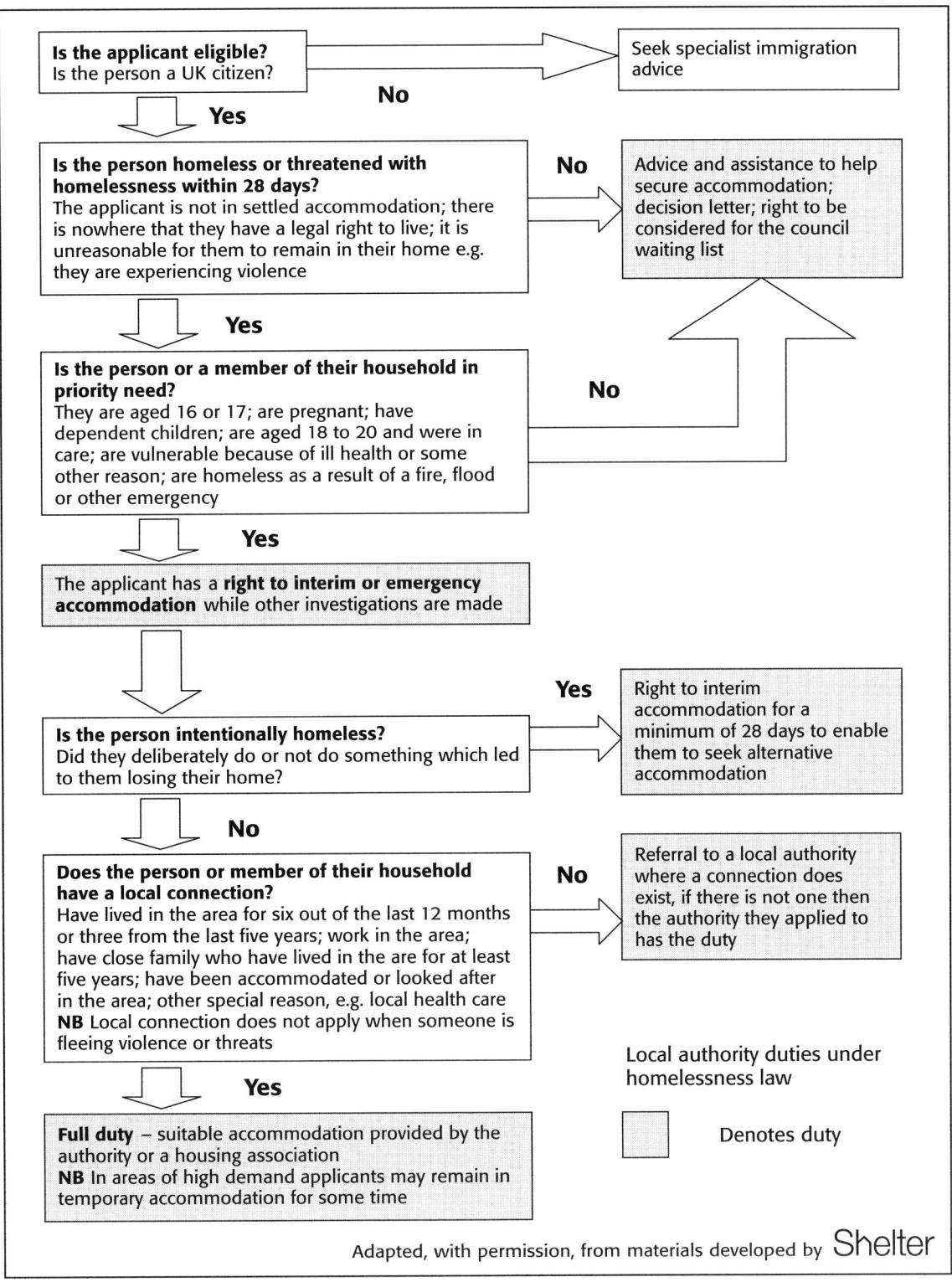

Adapted, with permission, from materials developed by Shelter

If your process flowchart looks like an octopus, it is probable that there are lots of unnecessary movements of people or material and you can act to simplify it.

Flowcharting is of particular use when a new way of working needs recording and publishing to all involved.

Mind mapping

Mind mapping is a technique that addresses the fact that we are conditioned during our education to make lists, work in categories, present things in order, be organised, be tidy, and be controlled. Yet when we start to think about an issue or a problem our thought process tends to fly off in many directions. The last thing we are is organised or tidy. If we do manage to stick to 'producing a list' or 'categorising our results' it usually stifles the thought process. Mind mapping allows us to let our mind go wherever it wants, but allows us to 'capture' the journey it has taken by drawing a map or picture.

A finished mind map looks quite like a tree. Not a family tree, which is organised and formal but a real tree which has grown in whatever direction it needed to grow and is not the same as any other tree in the world. Any mind map that you draw is unlikely to be the same as any other mind map drawn by any other person even though it may contain similar information.

To draw a mind map you choose a topic and write the topic down in the centre of a blank page, in a circle. Then, whatever comes into your mind next as you think about the topic you write in another circle and connect the two circles with a line. Then, if what you think about next relates to the second circle you attach it there, but if your mind has gone in a different direction you start another branch of the tree.

So, for example if I start to think about 'family' my mind might say 'Holidays' then 'Bois Soleil' and 'Beach' and 'Chris swimming' and 'Sarah lost'. Then it might jump to 'My Dad' for example, and I might think 'Bike ride' and then 'The War' and then 'Deaf' so my mind map would begin like this:

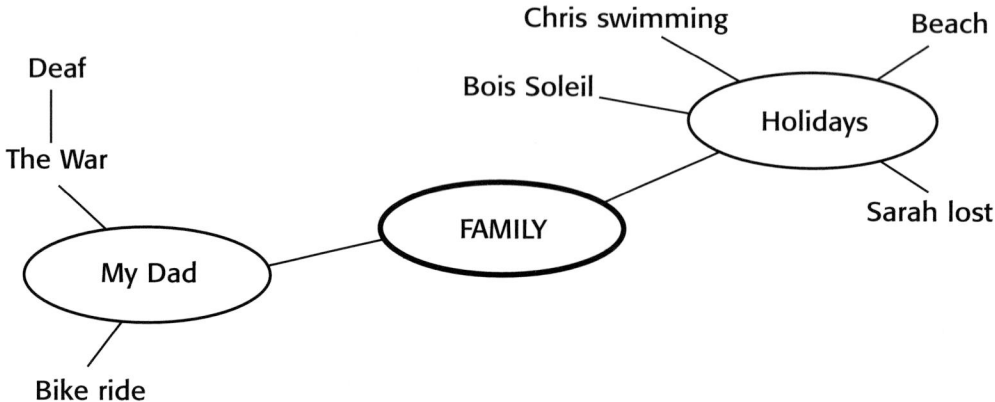

Figure 12.11

Mind mapping eercise
Choose a topic, let your mind run freely and try to capture your thoughts as they happen. Do not think in groups or in any structured way, just record things as they come into your mind linking them as your mind has linked them. When you have exhausted your thoughts you stop, but you can always return and add things later, following the same free thinking principles.

When you have finished the mind map there are other things that you can do. For example. On my map I might colour 'the war' and 'deaf and 'Sarah lost' in black as they are not happy thoughts. The rest might be in yellow as they are all happy memories. Or I could use a colour for Sarah things, another colour for Chris things and a third colour for Dad things. I can do whatever I like within reason.

The beauty of mind mapping is that there are no hard and fast rules. Mind mapping is a very useful technique that has the capability to help individuals to capture their thoughts without putting any restrictions on the thinking process. It can be a very useful tool in the problem solving toolbox.

The topic is vast so I recommend you read the book on the subject written by Tony Buzan. (see *The Mind Map Book* – Tony Buzan) Even if you never try the technique you will find that the book is mentally and visually stimulating.

Summary

To summarise, the problem solving process goes something like this:

Figure 12.12: The approach to a problem

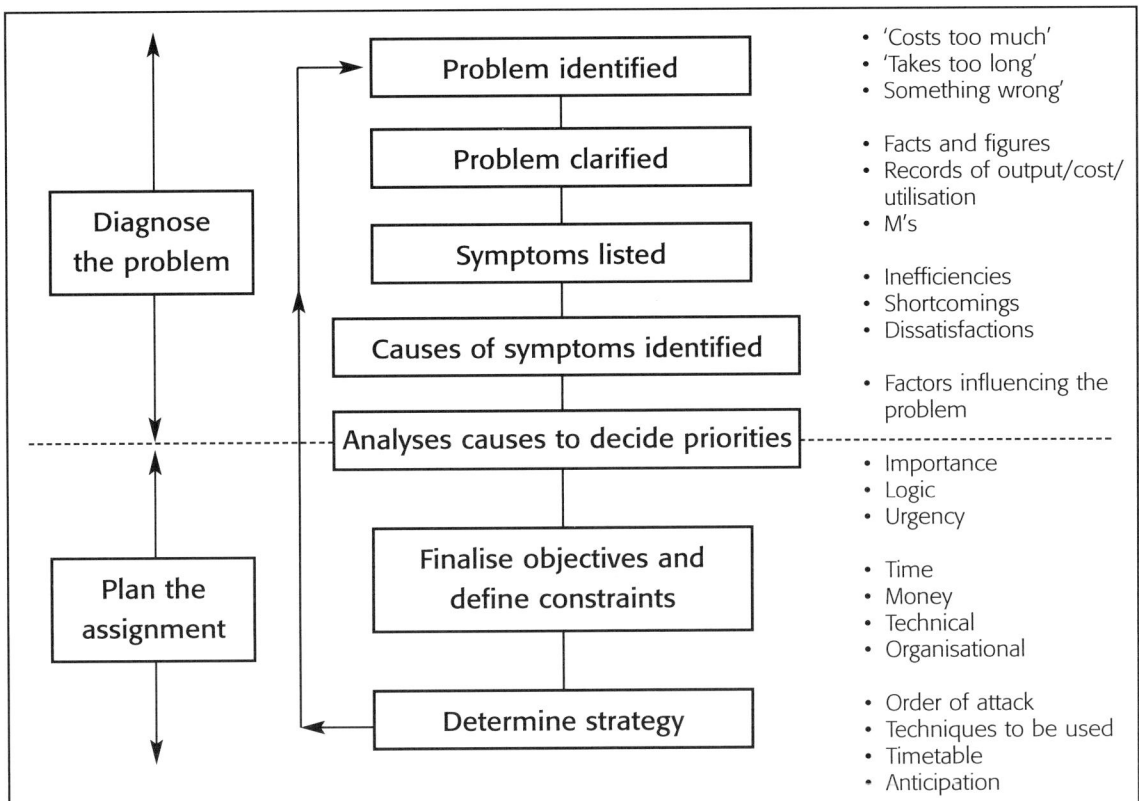

There are many other problem solving techniques available that we have not outlined in this chapter. If you try a number of techniques you can then settle on the ones that work best for you and for the particular project/problem on which you are working.

Remember you should be sufficiently flexible to try a new problem solving approach from time to time. The same applies to your approach to project management.

Final Thoughts

In the *Foreword* there is the story of a school Head who presided over a badly organised move to temporary premises. She vowed to learn from her mistakes – and did. The move back into the original, but by then re-furbished, premises, went very smoothly. The problem is that whilst getting things right at the second attempt is so much easier, it is nearly always more costly, in financial terms and more importantly in motivational terms. People do not enjoy being involved in badly organised or failed operations.

Getting things right at the first attempt is not as difficult as people imagine.

All of the information set out in this book has been gleaned from organisations that regularly get things right first time. To summarise what it is that they do:

- Firstly, they understand the importance of involving and communicating with all the interested parties in a project – and usually there are more interested parties than at first envisaged.

- They put considerable thought into the selection of the project team knowing that the wrong team rarely delivers the right results.

- They recognise that people need to have time allocated in order to work on projects – i.e. project participants need to be relieved of some of their day-to-day work in order to do their project work properly.

- They understand the value of formally assigning roles and responsibilities for various aspects of their projects.

- They spend time involving all the interested parties in the planning process, understanding that anticipation is the key to avoiding last minute panics.

- They set SMART goals.

- They communicate progress as the project unfolds – no one is kept in the dark.

- Six months or so after the project is completed they review the successes.

Good luck with your projects. Treat them like your children. Take them seriously. Watch over them. If you don't watch over them, worry about them, care about them – they will go off the rails.

Bibliography

Armstrong, M. (1993) *A Handbook of Management Techniques*. London, BCA.

Battersby, A. (1964) *Network Analysis for Planning and Scheduling*. Surrey, Macmillan.

Belbin, R.M. (1997) *Management Teams and Why they Succeed or Fail*. Butterworth Henemann.

Blanchard, K., Zigarmi, P. and Zigarmi, D. (1987) *Leadership and the One Minute Manager*. Glasgow, Collins.

Buzan, A. with Buzan, B. (1993) *The Mind Map Book*. London, BCA.

DeBono, E. (2000) *Six Thinking Hats*. London, Penguin.

Handy, C. (1993) *Understanding Organisations*. London, Penguin.

McGregor, D. (1967) *The Professional Manager*. London. McGraw Hill.

Myers, K.D. and Briggs, K. (1995) *Introduction to Type – Dynamics and Development*. Oxford, Psychological Press.

Rafferty, J. (1994) *Risk Analysis in Project Management*. London, E & FN Spon.

Reiss, G. (1992) *Project Management Demystified*. London, E & FN Spon.

Rust, J. and Golombok, S. (1999) *Modern Psychometrics – The Science of Psychological Assessment*. London, Routledge.